PREFACE
PREFACE
PREFACE

Physics. What is it? What is it to do with you? Does it affect you? Can you eat it? Is your life better off with or without it? What is it like to be a physicist? What do physicists do? How do they do it? Are physicists unusual people? Can you 'do' physics?

These questions cannot be answered in a sentence, or even a page of writing. It takes a book to *begin* to answer these questions—this book.

You learn a lot by asking questions, and then trying to answer them. You have already had ten questions on this page alone. There are plenty more questions on the pages that follow. Whenever you see a question mark—?—in this book, think about the question being asked and try to write an answer.

At the end of each chapter there are a few more questions: 'Further questions'. Some questions are to see whether you have understood what the chapter is about. Several questions have new ideas for you to think about. Many questions would be good for discussing with your teacher and friends. Several of the problems are quite challenging, to get you really thinking!

You also learn a lot by watching and copying other people. In this book you will meet (in photographs) four pupils of your age. Their names are Fiona, Jillian, Mike and Paul and they are there to show you how to carry out some of the experiments.

Enjoy using this book!

Andrew Lambert
Ilkley

ACKNOWLEDGMENTS

The author and publishers would like to thank the following for permission to reproduce copyright material.

Fig. 1.11   South of Scotland Electricity Board
Fig. 1.13   National Railway Museum
Fig. 1.15   North of Scotland Hydro-Electric Board
Fig. 1.23 (a)   Science Photo Library
Fig. 1.23 (b)   Philips Electronics
Fig. 1.23 (e)   Central office of Information (Crown Copyright)
Fig. 3.12   GEC Witton Kramer Ltd
Fig. 3.20   British Telecom
Fig. 4.5   B. T. Batsford Ltd
Fig. 4.8   (Crown Copyright) Science Museum, London
Fig. 4.11   Photo. Science Museum, London
Fig. 4.12   Stouffer Productions. Oxford Scientific Films. Animals Animals
Fig. 4.14 and Fig. 4.16   Fergus Davidson Associates Limited
Fig. 4.21   Dunlop Sports Company Limited
Fig. 5.4   Barnaby's Picture Library
Fig. 5.7   De Beers Consolidated Mines Limited
Fig. 5.8   Dr J. R. Fryer, Dept. of Chemistry, University of Glasgow
Fig. 5.20   John Cleare, Mountain Camera
Fig. 5.21   British Steel Corporation
Fig. 5.42   Photo. Science Museum, London
Fig. 6.15, Fig. 6.16 and Fig. 6.17   Olympus Optical Co Ltd
Fig. 6.50   Photography by Photolabs, Royal Observatory, Edinburgh
Fig. 6.51   Original negative by UK Schmidt Telescope Unit
Fig. 6.55   Yerkes Observatory Photograph
Fig. 6.57   (Crown Copyright) Science Museum, London
Fig. 6.62   Central Press Photos
Fig. 7.3 and Fig. 7.27   *Glasgow Herald/Evening Times* Photo Library
Fig. 7.4   (Crown Copyright) National Engineering Laboratory

The cover photograph was supplied by the Dunlop Sports Company Limited.

All other photographs are the copyright of the author.

CONTENTS

1

ENERGY ENERGY ENERGY

Fig. 1.1 This Land Rover needs fuel—petrol—to keep it moving

1.1 Introduction

Look at Fig. 1.1. Like any other vehicle, this Land Rover needs a **fuel** (petrol) to keep it going. Without a fuel the Land Rover will eventually stop working. Then we might have to think of a different way of moving it, such as in Fig. 1.2. You can imagine that if you were pushing this Land Rover you would soon feel as

Fig. 1.2 Another way of moving the Land Rover

exhausted as these children did. You would say you were running out of **energy**. You would need to replace your energy with your own sort of fuel—food (Fig. 1.3).

Physicists say that fuels store something called **energy**. This energy can be released to do useful things for us. If all the energy stored in each biscuit being eaten by the children in Fig. 1.3 was used to push the Land Rover, the children could push it for over a kilometre on level ground. Have you any idea why they would feel exhausted long before this distance had been covered?

Fig. 1.3 These children need a fuel as well

1

Energy is a *useful* idea to a physicist; it turns up in so many different disguises and in so many different places. People and machines make use of energy. That is why this introductory chapter is about energy. A lot of this chapter will probably remind you of things you already know; other things will be new. Later chapters in this book will look at some different kinds of energy in a little more detail.

The petrol that stores the energy to drive the Land Rover comes from oil—one of the **fossil fuels**. Why is it called a fossil fuel? A fossil fuel that was used earlier than oil is coal; Victorian engineers learned how to make use of the energy stored in coal to make steam locomotives move. Fig. 1.4 shows a

Victorian locomotive which is still going strong. You can do other useful things with the energy stored in coal apart from making things move along. You could use this energy for making electricity or lifting something, for example. The energy stored in a fuel can be turned into different *kinds* of energy.

1.2 Different kinds of energy

Look at the model steam engine in Fig. 1.5. In this model the fuel is methylated spirits. The energy stored in the fuel is certainly making the **pistons** and **flywheel** move, but the flywheel is coupled to a **dynamo** (or **generator**) which is making electricity. The energy stored in the fuel is being converted to **electrical energy**.

If possible, put together this equipment for yourself and examine it closely. You may realize that the paragraph above does not state all that is happening. It is rather more complicated. Look at the apparatus bit by bit, starting with the burning meths.

Fig. 1.4   *Lion*, built for the Liverpool and Manchester railway in 1838

Fig. 1.5   A model steam engine generating electricity

2

Fig. 1.6   Changing chemical energy to heat energy

Fig. 1.7   Changing heat energy to kinetic energy

As the meths burns (Fig. 1.6) there is a **chemical reaction** taking place. This happens with all fossil fuels when you burn them to release the stored energy. Fossil fuels store **chemical energy**. The chemical energy stored in the meths is certainly not making electrical energy straight away. It is making something hot—the water in the boiler. The water is gaining **heat energy**. This heat energy is changed into the 'movement' energy (or **kinetic energy**, to give it its proper name) of the pistons and flywheel (Fig. 1.7) which in turn is converted into the kinetic energy of the dynamo (Fig. 1.8). Here the energy is converted to electrical energy. But the story does not finish here. In the lamps (Fig. 1.9), the electrical energy is converted to **light energy** and more heat energy. Fig. 1.10 is a summary of all these energy changes.

Fig. 1.8   Changing kinetic energy to electrical energy

Fig. 1.9   Changing electrical energy to heat and light energy

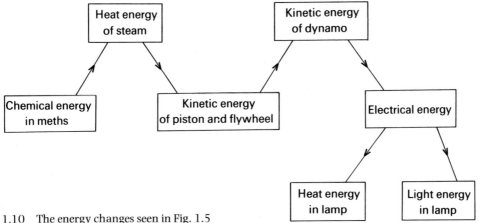

Fig. 1.10   The energy changes seen in Fig. 1.5

Fig. 1.11 The turbine hall of a power station

Exactly the same energy changes take place, on a much larger scale, inside a power station such as the one shown in Fig. 1.11. It is from such a power station that your home and school obtain their electrical energy. The steam piston engine is replaced by a **turbine**, but the energy changes are the same.

You may be able to see that an important feature of energy is the way you can change it from one form to another; this is when it is useful. Energy stored in a fuel is of no use until you 'release' it and change it to another form. It is rather like money in a bank account. You cannot eat it, clothe yourself in it or shelter under it. It is only useful when you transfer the money to someone else, and exchange it for food, clothing or shelter.

In what ways do you change the electrical energy that comes into your home or school from the power station?

1.3 Gravitational energy

Another use for the steam engine is shown in Fig. 1.12 where it is lifting Beatrice (our resident mouse) from the floor to the bench. Assemble this apparatus for yourself, if possible (although you will have to find something to take the place of Beatrice). Beatrice is *gaining* energy as she gets

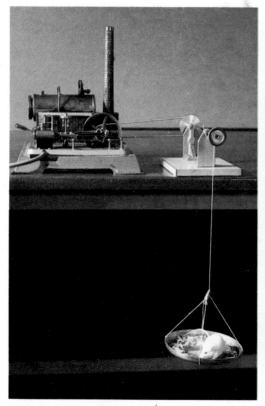

Fig. 1.12 Going up!

higher. She has more energy on the bench than on the floor.

The energy that Beatrice had on the bench is sometimes called 'position' energy, sometimes called 'uphill' energy. The proper name is **gravitational energy** or, better, **gravitational potential energy**.

4

Fig. 1.13   The stationary winding engine from Swannington, now in the National Railway Museum

The same energy changes took place when the machinery shown in Fig. 1.13 was used at Swannington, in Leicestershire, for hauling loaded wagons up a hill in the nineteenth century. Steam engines were first used as pumping engines to pump water out of mines, thus increasing the gravitational potential energy of the water.

It should be possible to change Beatrice's gravitational potential energy to electrical energy using the apparatus illustrated in Fig. 1.14, but when this was tried it would not work—Beatrice just stayed swinging in the air. Can you think of a good reason why the experiment illustrated in Fig. 1.14 will not work?

On a much larger scale, water which is stored in a reservoir high up on a hill can rush down the hill and drive a turbine to make electricity. This is what is happening in the **hydroelectric power station** in Fig. 1.15.

Fig. 1.14   Why is no electrical energy generated?

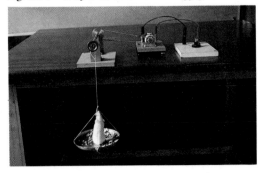

Fig. 1.15   A hydroelectric power station. The storage reservoir is on the other side of the mountain

1.4   Potential energy

You have just met the word 'potential'. It means 'stored'. Fuels store chemical energy, so chemical energy is a member of the **potential energy family**. Gravitational energy is stored energy—the water in the reservoir has a store of energy which is transformed into electrical energy when it falls down the hill. So gravitational energy belongs to the potential energy group.

Fig. 1.16 shows another example of the potential energy group. What name would you give to this energy? What energy changes will take place when the catapult is released?

Make a list of all the different sorts of energy you have met so far in this book. Add to your list any other sorts of energy you can think of.

Fig. 1.16   What sort of energy is stored in the catapult?

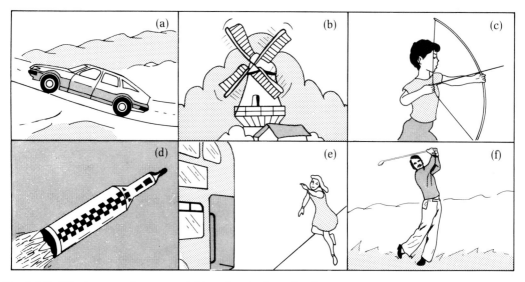

Fig. 1.17   What energy changes are taking place in these sketches?

Look at the sketches in Fig. 1.17. Write down what energy changes you think are happening in each case.

1.5   Light and radiation energy

One kind of energy which you probably included in your list is **light energy**. There is a little more to this than first meets the eye (literally)!

White light is made up of many different colours—the colours of the rainbow in Fig. 1.18. You can split a beam of white light into these colours using a prism, as shown in Fig. 1.19. You can *see* the different parts of the light. There are also some electronic devices which can 'see' the light. For example, a **light-dependent resistor** will let more electricity through it when there is light falling on it.

Fig. 1.18   A rainbow

Fig. 1.19   A prism can be used to split light from the slide projector into the colours of the rainbow

Fig. 1.20 A simple electric circuit containing a light-dependent resistor

Connect the simple circuit shown in Fig. 1.20. Check that the electric meter shows more current flowing when there is light on the light-dependent resistor than when there is not. Try putting the resistor in the **spectrum** (Fig. 1.21) and note the current.

Now put the resistor just beyond the red end of the spectrum as in Fig. 1.22 and note the current again. If there is still quite a large current in the circuit there must still be some energy arriving on the

Fig. 1.21 The light-dependent resistor in the visible spectrum

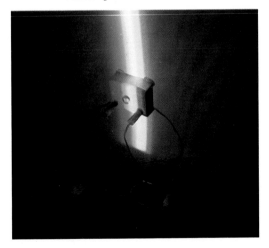

Fig. 1.22 The light-dependent resistor just beyond the red end of the spectrum

resistor that you cannot see but which the resistor *can* 'see'. This energy is called **infrared radiation**. Light is sometimes called **visible radiation**. Radiation energy is important because there are so many members of the **radiation family**.

The photographs in Fig. 1.23 give some clues to the other members of the radiation family. Write down the kinds of radiation energy that these photographs suggest to you.

7

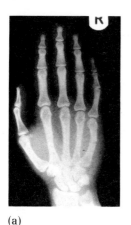
(a)

(b)

(c)

(d)

(e)

(f)

(g)

Fig. 1.23　What members of the radiation family do these photographs suggest to you?

1.6　Infrared radiation and heat

It is worth investigating infrared radiation a little further. Hot things are good at making infrared radiation. The heater in Fig. 1.24 is converting heat energy to radiation energy. Some of this radiation is visible, but most of it is infrared.

Hold your hand near a heater, as in the photograph. (It is best if your hand is behind a protective screen in which there is a hole.) Your hand feels warm. The radiation energy is being *absorbed* by your hand and *converted* into heat energy.

Many people are confused about this. The heater is *not* giving out heat energy. It is giving out radiation energy, and this is changed to heat energy when it is absorbed by your hand.

Are all kinds of surfaces equally good at absorbing radiation energy and converting it to heat energy? Try this simple experiment. Clench your fist and make it wet. Ask someone to put a piece of aluminium leaf over your clenched fist as

Fig. 1.24   This hand is changing the radiation energy falling on it into heat energy

Fig. 1.25   Cover your hand with aluminium leaf

in Fig. 1.25. Hold your fist in the same place as before. Is there less infrared radiation being converted to heat energy than before, or more, or the same?

Now paint the leaf black with carbon black mixed in meths. Let it dry, and then put your hand back near the heater. Does the black surface make any difference? Which sort of surface is best at absorbing infrared radiation and converting it to heat?

1.7   Energy does not get lost

This chapter has gone into some detail about energy *changes*, but at no point

have we said that energy was 'used up'. This is simply because it is not used up! This is a very important idea in physics—energy may change from one form to another, but it is not used up. This idea goes under the title of **the law of conservation of energy**.

Why, then, is there great concern in the world about running out of energy—the 'energy crisis'? How can we run out of energy if energy is not used up? The answer is, we will not! But we *will* run out of energy that we can put to use. In particular, we will sooner or later run out of fossil fuels.

Look back at the various energy changes you have written down or which are illustrated in this chapter. Notice how often heat energy is made. Not only are there cases where fuels are burnt to make heat, electrical energy can be converted to heat energy (where, for example?) and friction between moving surfaces results in heat energy. (Try feeling a blunt drill after drilling a hole with it.)

This heat energy spreads itself out thinly everywhere. We say it 'escapes' or 'gets lost'. This is not strictly true—it is still there, but thinly spread out and it is not possible to get this heat energy back again to do anything useful. The branch of physics that deals with this in greater detail is called **thermodynamics**.

We are burning our stocks of useful chemical energy found in fossil fuels to make thinly spread out, useless heat energy. Engines like petrol engines or steam turbines *have* to throw away some heat energy to the atmosphere in order to work at all. What about the heat loss from houses? Does heat *have* to be wasted here?

How serious do you think this problem is? Try to find out how long the world's oil is expected to last. How old will you be when the oil runs out? Coal is expected to last a little longer. How much longer? What will you do when they both run out? Do we need oil and coal for anything apart from energy?

Now that you have finished studying this chapter on energy, there are a number of things you should know or be able to do.

1 You should:
   a) know about several different kinds of energy;
   b) be able to describe some examples of energy changes from one form to another;
   c) know about the members of the radiation family;
   d) know that energy is not lost—it is conserved;
   e) realize that the Earth has a very limited store of fossil fuels.
2 You should know what each of the following is, or what each does:

energy
fuel
fossil
chemical reaction
piston
flywheel
generator
turbine

hydroelectric
   power
light-dependent
   resistor
spectrum
infrared radiation
visible radiation
dynamo

3 These are some of the other words that have been used in this chapter. You should know what each word means:

exhausted
introductory
release
assemble
transform

absorb
convert
crisis
conserve

FURTHER QUESTIONS

1 Write down what *sort* of energy is stored in the following:
   a) compressed spring b) a biscuit
   c) petrol d) a car battery
   e) water in a high dam
   f) a moving car g) TNT

2 A *transducer* is any device which changes energy from one form to another. Suggest a suitable transducer for each one of the following energy changes:
   a) sound to electrical energy
   b) electrical energy to sound
   c) chemical to electrical energy
   d) chemical to light energy
   e) elastic potential to kinetic energy
   f) chemical energy to kinetic energy
   g) electrical energy to light energy
   h) light energy to electrical energy

3 Write down the energy changes which take place in the following descriptions of events. Say what sort of energy is involved at each stage and where that energy is. For example, for a man digging a ditch: chemical energy stored in the man's muscles is converted to gravitational potential energy of the soil lifted from the ditch.
   a) Sprinter running down a race track.
   b) Mainspring in a watch driving the hands round.
   c) High jumper running up to bar, jumping over and landing in sand.
   d) Aircraft being catapulted from an aircraft carrier's deck.
   e) Water in reservoir running down to hydroelectric power station, which makes electricity.
   f) Radio waves being sent from transmitter, picked up by aerial on radio, person listens to radio programme.

4 Why do many people who inhabit hot countries wear white clothing, and why are tropical suits white? (Your answer should include the words 'radiation energy'.)

5 Try to find out (from a library, for instance) who invented the following, and when:
   a) steam pumping engine
   b) diesel engine c) jet engine
   d) motor car e) steam locomotive
   f) electric motor

2

ELECTRIC CIRCUITS
ELECTRIC CIRCUITS

ELECTRIC CIRCUITS

2.1   Introduction

It is very hard to escape from electrical energy in your everyday life. It is used in so many different ways and it tends to be taken for granted. It is clean, convenient and probably available in your home at the flick of a switch. Look at Fig. 2.1. Here are three ways of providing energy to move a railway train. Which is the cleanest, and the most convenient? This cleanliness is a little deceptive. Why? Look at Fig. 2.2.

Fig. 2.1(a)   Southern Railways steam locomotive *Lord Nelson* at Settle, N. Yorkshire

Fig. 2.1(b)   A class 86 electric locomotive at Shap, in Cumbria

Fig. 2.1(c)   An Intercity-125 express at Leeds station

11

Fig. 2.2 A power station generating electricity

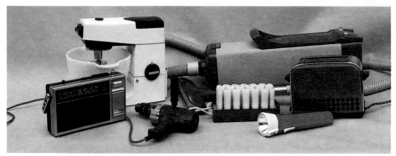

Fig. 2.3   Some things which use electricity. What other things can you think of?

Some of the everyday objects that make use of electricity are shown in Fig. 2.3. Write down a few other things that make use of electricity and which are not illustrated in this photograph.

This chapter introduces some of the important ideas that are necessary to understand how, and why, some of the things shown in Fig. 2.3 work. Not *all* the ideas you need are in this chapter. Electric motors, for example, are looked at in Chapter 3.

There is another reason for knowing about electricity. When you come to look at atoms in some detail, you will find that you need to understand a little about electricity in order to understand atoms.

Fig. 2.4   A small part of a large electric circuit

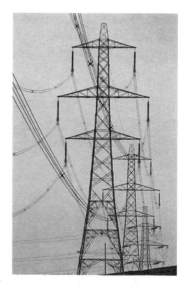

2.2   Simple electric circuits

Electric circuits come in all shapes and sizes. Fig. 2.4 shows part of the large but relatively simple circuit that carries our electricity round the country, while Fig. 2.5 shows the very complicated circuit to be found inside a modern **microcomputer**.

Fig. 2.5   Part of the inside of a microcomputer

Each of the small pieces of black plastic which look as if they are standing on legs is an **integrated circuit**. Fig. 2.6 shows what is inside one of them. The tiny piece of silicon in the middle has thousands of parts, or 'components' on it. You can just see the fine gold wires that connect this 'chip' to the feet (or pins) of the assembly.

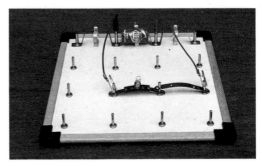

Fig. 2.7   One kind of apparatus for investigating electric circuits

Fig. 2.8   A different set of apparatus for investigating electric circuits

Fig. 2.6   The 'chip' inside one of the integrated circuits in the previous photograph

Many of the same basic ideas are used in both the circuits illustrated on page 12. You can find out about these ideas using the simple items of apparatus shown in Fig. 2.7 and Fig. 2.8. Both circuits are the same, but different apparatus is used to support the batteries and lamps to keep the circuit neat and tidy. This is important. You will have little hope of understanding what is happening if your circuit looks like knitting after the cat has been at it!

Fig. 2.7 shows the neatest layout, with all the items supported on a **circuit board**. Fig. 2.8 illustrates a separate holder for the batteries, with the lamps supported on a **clip component holder**. Your school might use one of these methods, or it might have one of its own. The illustrations in this chapter will usually show the circuit board method as in Fig. 2.7. Notice that the photograph shows a complete, continuous path for the electricity, starting at one end of the battery, going through the lamp, and returning to the other end of the battery.

Set up the simple circuit shown in Fig. 2.7 for yourself and check that the lamp only lights up if there *is* a complete path. Then answer the following questions and carry out the simple experiments listed below.

1 How do you *know* there is electricity flowing round your simple circuit? (We call this flow of electricity an **electric current**.)
2 How can you tell roughly *how much* current there is?
3 Take your battery out of its holder and put it back in the other way round. Does your lamp light equally well?

13

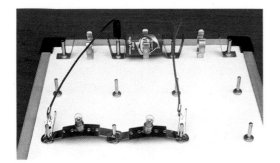

Fig. 2.9 A battery with two lamps in series

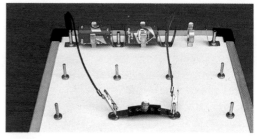

Fig. 2.10 Two batteries with one lamp

Fig. 2.11 Why is it not a good idea to connect this circuit?

4 Use your battery with *two* lamps, arranged one after the other as in Fig. 2.9. Does this make any difference to the brightness of the lamps? What can you write down about the electric current in this second circuit compared to the current in the first circuit? When the lamps are arranged one after the other in this way we say they are **in series**.

5 Now use *two* batteries together, first with one lamp (Fig. 2.10), then with two lamps, and finally with three lamps in series. You could have the batteries both facing the same way, as in Fig. 2.10, or one facing the opposite way to the other. In each case, compare the brightness of the lamps, and the electric current that is flowing, with the first circuit you made (Fig. 2.7). It will be best if you record your results in a table like the one opposite.

6 After using two batteries, try using three batteries, first with two lamps and then with three lamps. Do not use three batteries with just one lamp as in Fig. 2.11. Why not? Record your results from these experiments in your table.

You can write a summary of the main points from these simple experiments by copying out the following paragraph. Some gaps have been left in the paragraph. Fill these in, choosing the correct word or words from the list which follows. You do not need to use all the words in the list.

'If there is an electric circuit with a

Number of batteries	Number of lamps	Brightness of lamps*
1	2	
2 facing same way	1	
2 facing opposite ways	1	

*Compared to one lamp lit by one battery.

number of lamps in series, the lamps will be 'normally bright' if there are as many batteries as there are lamps. If there are more batteries than there are lamps, then the lamps will be _____ and if there are fewer batteries than lamps then the lamps will be _____. For this to be true, the batteries will be _____.'

Fill in the gaps with words from the following list:

normally bright/brighter than normal/dimmer than normal/unlit/each of a dif-

14

ferent brightness/all facing the same way/facing in opposite directions.

2.3 Electricity and heat energy

In the last section you judged how much current was flowing round your circuit by the brightness of the lamps. But why does a lamp light up at all? Look carefully inside the lamp, and notice the very fine wire through which the current flows as it goes through the lamp. This fine wire is called the **filament**. Try to find out which metal it is made from.

Use three batteries to send current through a thin piece of wire made from eureka (eureka is an alloy of copper and nickel). Fig. 2.12 shows one possible way of doing this. Carefully feel the wire to find out if it is becoming warm. The shorter the wire, the warmer it becomes—try this with your wire. The filament in an electric lamp is a very short, thin piece of wire that becomes so hot that it glows white. Electrical energy is being converted into heat energy. This heat energy is then converted to radiation energy, as you saw in Chapter 1. Some of this radiation energy is visible (it is light!) and the rest is infrared radiation. An electric lamp is not very efficient at making light energy—most of the electrical energy is converted into infrared radiation, and only 5% becomes visible radiation.

Fig. 2.12   What does an electric current do to this piece of wire?

Fig. 2.13   This iron makes use of the heating effect of an electric current

You have just looked at one of the *effects* of an electric current—one of the things that an electric current *does*—an electric current can make a wire hot. This is called the **heating effect** of an electric current. Fig. 2.13 shows one common thing that makes use of this heating effect of electricity. Write down as many other things which you can think of that make use of the heating effect of electricity.

2.4 Fuses

The heating effect that you have just investigated can be dangerous as well as useful. Something that is connected to an electricity supply might become faulty so that too much current starts to flow along the wires. They might become too hot and start a fire. A **fuse** is used to disconnect the circuit from the supply before the wires become too hot. How does a fuse work?

In the last experiment you passed an electric current along a fine piece of wire, and that wire became hot. Repeat the experiment, this time using a very fine, short piece of wire taken from a piece of steel wool. This time the wire becomes very hot and melts. This is how a fuse works. It is a fine piece of wire that becomes very hot and melts thus breaking the circuit, when too much electric current flows through it.

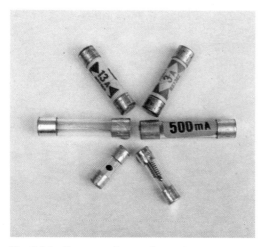

Fig. 2.14   Fuses are designed to melt at a wide
variety of different currents

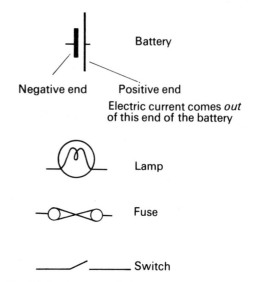

Fig. 2.15   Circuit symbols

Fig. 2.14 shows several fuses, designed to melt at different current amounts. Why do you think they are enclosed in a case, which, as you can see from the photograph, is sometimes made of glass?

The same thing will happen to the filament of a lamp as happens to a fuse if too much current is passed through it. This is why you were told not to use three batteries with one lamp in your earlier experiments (Fig. 2.11).

2.5   Circuit symbols

Physicists have agreed on certain signs, or **symbols**, to represent the various items used in electric circuits so that it is easy to make a record of what you are doing when you are investigating and drawing diagrams of electric circuits. All scientists use these symbols so that they can understand each other's work quickly and easily.

The symbols for a battery, lamp, fuse and switch are shown in Fig. 2.15. Later in this chapter you will meet some other symbols which, like those on this page, should be learned.

Fig. 2.16 shows a circuit diagram using these symbols for the circuit shown in Fig. 2.10. Notice how all the connections are

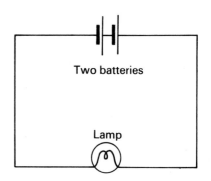

Fig. 2.16   The circuit diagram for the circuit
shown in Fig. 2.10

drawn with straight lines. (Always use a ruler!) This makes it much simpler to read the circuit.

2.6   Series and parallel circuits

When you were investigating simple electric circuits earlier, you arranged your lamps one after the other, in series, as in Fig. 2.9. But there is another way of arranging two lamps to be lit by one battery. This is illustrated in Fig. 2.17. Fig. 2.18 shows the circuit diagram. These lamps are arranged **in parallel**. In this section you are going to investigate

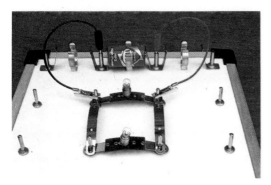

Fig. 2.17   A battery and two lamps in parallel

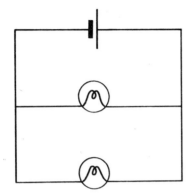

Fig. 2.18   The circuit diagram for Fig. 2.17

the differences between series and parallel circuits.

Assemble the series circuit first, as shown in the circuit diagram in Fig. 2.19. This is the circuit illustrated in Fig. 2.9.

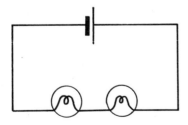

Fig. 2.19   A battery with two lamps in series

How bright are the lamps compared with a circuit where one battery lights one lamp only? (Look back at your earlier work.)

Suppose one lamp breaks. What happens to the other one? (Do not actually break a lamp! Unscrew it from its holder instead.)

Now assemble the parallel circuit shown in Fig. 2.17. How bright are the lamps this time? Suppose one lamp is broken or disconnected. What happens to the other lamp? Which circuit do you think is better for lighting lamps? Give a reason for your answer.

How do you think the lights in your home are wired—in series or in parallel? How do you know?

2.7   Using an ammeter

So far, you have judged how much current is flowing in your circuit by the brightness of the lamps. Do you think this is a very good way of judging the amount of electric current? Give a reason for your answer.

Another way of measuring an electric current is to use an instrument called an **ammeter**. Ammeters come in many shapes and sizes. One typical ammeter is shown in Fig. 2.20. It has a needle which moves over a scale to show how much current there is. There is a red terminal for the current to go *into* the meter, and a black terminal for the current to come *out* of the meter. On some meters these terminal are marked '+' and '−'. The ammeter shown in Fig. 2.20 reads up to a maximum of 1 **ampere**, or 1 **amp**, which is how we usually refer to the unit of electric current. The photograph shows the ammeter reading 0.6 amp.

Fig. 2.20   A typical ammeter. It is reading a
current of 0.6 amp

17

The ammeter shown in Fig. 2.21 is known as a **dual-range meter**; the current goes in the red terminal but can be taken out of either of the black terminals. The meter will read to a maximum of 1 amp or 5 amps depending on which black terminal is used.

Fig. 2.21   A dual range ammeter, also reading 0.6 amp

Instead of having a needle moving over a scale, some meters show the current directly with numbers, like the meter in Fig. 2.22. This is called a **digital ammeter**. Digital instruments are becoming more and more common. One advantage is that they are more robust than the older **analogue meters** shown in the previous two photographs.

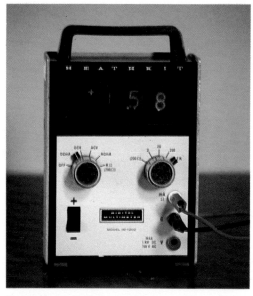

Fig. 2.22   A digital ammeter

Can you think of anything where it is now fairly common to find a digital version rather than the analogue version?

Fig. 2.23   The circuit symbol for an ammeter

The symbol for an ammeter is shown in Fig. 2.23.

You may need to be shown how to use the scale of the ammeter that you are using if it is not as simple as the one shown in Fig. 2.20. Make sure you understand how to use the scale of your ammeter.

Fig. 2.24 shows an ammeter correctly connected in a simple electric circuit, and Fig. 2.25 shows the circuit diagram. Connect this circuit for yourself, to make sure that you can put an ammeter into an electric circuit correctly and that you are able to read the scale.

Fig. 2.24   An ammeter correctly connected into a simple electric circuit

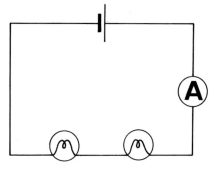

Fig. 2.25   The circuit diagram for the circuit shown in the previous photograph

2.8 Measuring the current in different parts of a circuit

Now that you know about ammeters, you can have a closer look at what happens to an electric current as it goes round a circuit. Connect the simple circuit shown in Fig. 2.26, with your ammeter measuring the current coming *out* of the battery. Write down how much current the ammeter shows is coming from your battery.

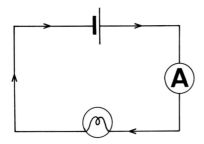

Fig. 2.26 A circuit to measure the current leaving the battery

Now change the position of your ammeter so that it measures the current returning to your battery, as in Fig. 2.27. Write down the reading on the ammeter this time.

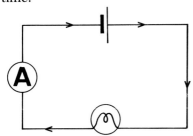

Fig. 2.27 Measuring the current returning to the battery

What do you notice about the two readings? Write down one or two sentences saying what *conclusion* you can come to from doing this simple experiment.

Next investigate a slightly bigger circuit, as in Fig. 2.28. There are three possible places where you can put your ammeter; these are marked with an '×' in the diagram. Put your ammeter at each

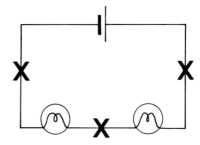

Fig. 2.28 Use an ammeter to measure the current at each of the places marked 'X'

place in turn to measure the current, and write down the readings on your ammeter.

What conclusion do you come to from this experiment? Is it the same conclusion that you came to after investigating the first circuit?

If you have time, try one or two other series circuits to see if the same thing happens. It is worth trying at least one circuit with two batteries so that you can measure the current between the batteries (Fig. 2.29). You may have to think very carefully about how you are going to put your ammeter *between* the two batteries. All the current that comes out of one battery must go through your ammeter before it goes into the other battery.

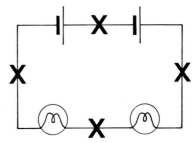

Fig. 2.29 What is the current at each of the places marked 'X' in this circuit?

2.9 The water circuit board

The results of your work in the last section may well seem a little puzzling—the electricity does not seem to get used up; it just keeps going round and round the circuit. (I hope you came to

19

that conclusion! If not, have another look at your experiments and your results to see if you agree.) If electricity does not get used up, why do you need a battery? Certainly not to *make* electricity.

One problem in trying to sort out the answer to this question is that you cannot *see* electricity; you can only see what it does. Some people find that this makes it a little difficult to understand what is going on. To help you, look at something that behaves in a *similar* way to electricity that you *can* see. One example is water flowing through pipes in a **water circuit**.

Fig. 2.30 shows a water circuit. The pump at the bottom pumps water round the pipes. The pipes divide into two narrow pipes at the top. The water flowing into the funnel makes a whirlpool; the deeper the whirlpool, the faster the flow of water. The water in the photograph has been coloured so that you can see it.

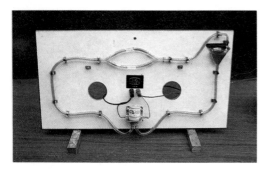

Fig. 2.30   A water circuit

Draw a diagram of this water circuit and mark on your diagram the part of the water circuit that you think does the *same* job as the battery does in an electric circuit. Also mark on your diagram the part of the water circuit that corresponds to a lamp. What do you think the funnel corresponds to in an electric circuit?

Which of the electric circuits in Fig. 2.31 is the one that is most similar to this water circuit?

Obviously, the same amount of water is flowing out of the pump as flows back in, in just the same way as the same amount

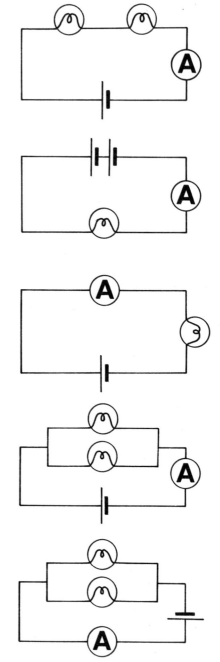

Fig. 2.31   Which electric circuit is most like the water circuit shown in Fig. 2.30?

of electricity flowed out of your battery as flowed back in again. The pump is not *making* water. A battery does not *make* electricity. The pump gives energy to the water so that it can get round the circuit, especially through the thin pipes at the top. The water is already in the pipes; it does not have to be made. In the same way, a battery gives electricity *energy* to get round the circuit, especially to get through the filament in a lamp.

What do you think happens to the energy of the electricity as it goes through the lamp?

Does this suggest that electricity is in the wires all the time, waiting for something to provide it with energy?

Scientists say that the water circuit is an **analogy** for an electric circuit. Of course, it is not absolutely identical—after all, water is not electricity! Scientists often make use of analogies to help them explain things they do not understand very well in terms of things they do understand.

2.10 Investigating parallel circuits

When you measured the current in different places in a series circuit, you found that electric current is not used up, but is the same wherever you measure it. It is now time for you to find out whether the same sort of rule applies to parallel circuits. There are two separate investigations that you could carry out.

First investigation

Connect the simple circuit shown in Fig. 2.32. It is helpful if the batteries used for this investigation are fairly new. Write down how much current is flowing. Then, without disconnecting this circuit,

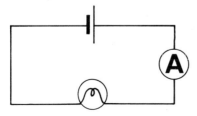

Fig. 2.32   Measuring the current going to one lamp

add a second lamp parallel to the first (Fig. 2.33) and record the new current. Does the brightness of the first lamp change very much?

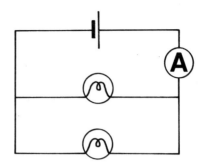

Fig. 2.33   Measuring the current going to two parallel lamps

Finally, add a third lamp parallel to the other two (Fig. 2.34) and write down how much current is flowing from the battery in this third circuit.

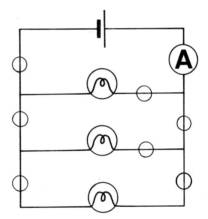

Fig. 2.34   Measuring the current going to three parallel lamps

The results of this experiment are important. When you investigated series circuits you found that adding more lamps to the circuit *decreased* the current coming from the batteries and the lamps became *dimmer*. With a parallel circuit, adding more lamps in parallel to the others *increases* the current coming from the batteries and the lamps stay at much the same brightness. Connecting a second lamp parallel to the first does not seem to

21

affect the current in the first lamp, but the batteries *also* have to send current to the second lamp, so the total current coming from the batteries is more than it was before. Fig. 2.35 illustrates this important idea.

Suppose the battery sends 0.3 A through the lamp in this circuit

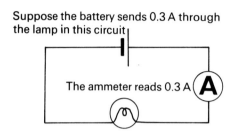

The ammeter reads 0.3 A (A)

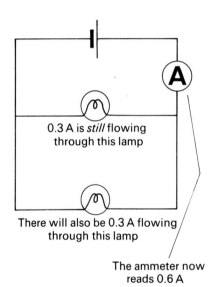

0.3 A is *still* flowing through this lamp

There will also be 0.3 A flowing through this lamp

The ammeter now reads 0.6 A

Fig. 2.35

It might help you if you think of each parallel circuit as a totally independent circuit. Three lamps in parallel could be wired as in Fig. 2.36. (This would not be a very economical way of using wire, though.) The battery will supply whatever current is needed in each circuit regardless of what it is supplying to any other circuit.

This last statement is not quite true—a battery cannot go on supplying more and more current indefinitely—there is a

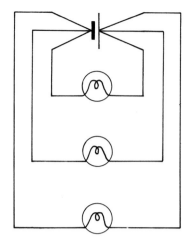

Fig. 2.36   Another way of wiring three parallel lamps

limit. For a new U2 battery the current is limited to about 2 amps. For a car battery the maximum current will be nearer 100 amps.

The lights in your house are wired in parallel (how do you know?). When you switch on a light, the **mains supply** provides the current for that light as well as continuing to provide whatever current it was supplying to other lights.

Second investigation

You can check on some of the ideas from the first investigation into parallel circuits by measuring the current in different branches of a parallel circuit. Connect again the circuit shown in Fig. 2.34 and use your ammeter to measure, in turn, the current at each place marked with a circle. Make a copy of the circuit diagram and write down on your copy the current you measure at each place.

You will have to think very carefully about how to connect your ammeter into your circuit so that you measure the current you want to measure. Figs 2.37 and 2.38 might help you.

Each time you make a measurement, unscrew each of the three lamps in turn to see if this has any effect on the current through your ammeter.

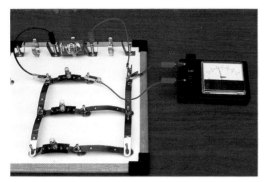

Fig. 2.37 This is how to connect the ammeter to measure the current through one of the three parallel lamps in Fig. 2.34

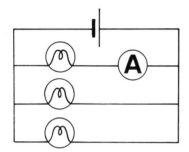

Fig. 2.38 The circuit diagram for the circuit shown in the previous photograph

Write a summary of this investigation. Write a few words about the results you obtain, and any conclusion to which you come.

2.11 Insulators, conductors and resistors

Some substances do not seem to conduct electricity at all—they are called electrical **insulators**. It would be very difficult to make an electric circuit without insulators, wouldn't it? (Why?) Write down the names of half a dozen insulators.

Substances which *do* conduct electricity are called **conductors**. Are you a conductor of electricity? Try a simple experiment to find out. Connect yourself in series with a battery and ammeter in the same way as Fiona has done in the photograph (Fig. 2.40). Fiona found *no*

Fig. 2.39 An insulator on an overhead electricity pylon

Fig. 2.40 Does Fiona conduct electricity?

current was going through her. What about you?

This result is a little strange. Fiona can get an electric shock as a result of an electric current passing through her. Perhaps only a very small current passes through Fiona (and you?)—too small to show on the ammeter. If this is so, we would say that Fiona conducts electricity, but she is not a very good conductor. Another way of saying this is to say that she has a *high resistance* to electricity, or that she has a high **electrical resistance**.

How could you modify your experiment to investigate whether a small current *does* flow through you? Your experiment must still be *safe*. Do not try it until your teacher has told you that what you propose to do *is* safe.

A metal wire is a much better conductor (it has much less resistance) than you. But are all metals equally good? To find out, connect a simple circuit using a battery, lamp and ammeter and write down how much current there is. Then include in your circuit 1 metre of copper wire; Fig. 2.41 shows you one way to do this. The circuit diagram is shown next to the photograph.

Fig. 2.41   A simple electric circuit which includes a copper 'resistor'

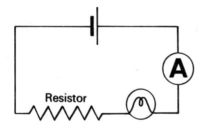

Fig. 2.42   The circuit diagram for Fig. 2.41

The copper wire is represented by the zig-zag line. This is the symbol for a **resistor** (which is something put into a circuit to resist the flow of electric current). You can add this symbol to your list of symbols. You may come across an alternative symbol for a resistor, which is the box shown in Fig. 2.43.

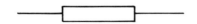

Fig. 2.43   An alternative symbol for a resistor

Does the copper wire make any difference to the current in your electric circuit?

Now use 1 metre of eureka wire of the same thickness in place of the copper wire. Does this make any difference to the current?

Which metal do you think has the greater resistance, or were they both the same?

Another investigation into resistance is shown in Fig. 2.44. Stretch 1 metre of thin eureka wire on the bench. Holding it at each end with a clip component holder is quite convenient. The 'crocodile clip' can be slid up or down the wire so that the length of eureka wire that is actually in the circuit can be changed. Connect the circuit and slide the clip along the wire. Write down what happens to the lamp and the reading on the ammeter. Try to explain *why* the current changes in the way it does.

Fig. 2.44   What happens to the electric current in this circuit when you use different lengths of wire?

What you have just made is a simple **variable resistor** (or **rheostat** to use the alternative name). The possible symbols for a variable resistor are shown in Fig. 2.45. Most variable resistors are a little more compact than the one you have just made. Not all of them are, though. Those which have to handle a lot of power tend to be quite big. A typical variable resistor is shown in Fig. 2.46. Try to work out for yourself how to connect this into a circuit. The photograph of the inside of the variable resistor (Fig. 2.47) might help you.

What do you think a variable resistor might be used for in practice? Write down two or three things you can think of.

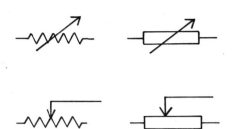

Fig. 2.45   Possible symbols for a variable resistor

Fig. 2.46   A variable resistor

Fig. 2.47   Inside the variable resistor in the previous photograph

2.12   More circuits

Here are some more circuits for you to investigate. Try to work out what will happen in these circuits before you connect them.

1 Fig. 2.48. What do you think will happen to the reading on the ammeter and the brightness of the lamp when the switch S is closed?

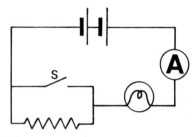

Fig. 2.48

2 Fig. 2.49. What do you think will happen to the brightness of lamps X and Y, and to the reading on the ammeter, as the variable resistor is changed from a small to a large resistance?

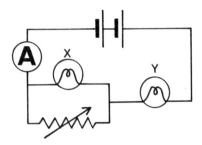

Fig. 2.49

3 In the circuit shown in Fig. 2.50 the lamps will not light. Why not? What will happen if you connect a piece of wire between points A and B?

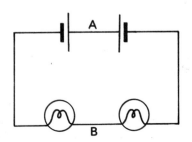

Fig. 2.50

25

4 The circuit in Fig. 2.51 enables a light to be turned on or off from either of two switches. For example, a light on a staircase can be turned on or off from either the top or bottom of the stairs. Try to work out for yourself how the circuit works. Try to make a model of this circuit using the parts from your electric circuit apparatus.

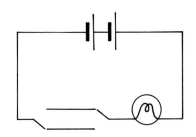

Fig. 2.51

SUMMARY

Now that you have finished studying this chapter on electric circuits, there are a number of things you should know or be able to do.

1 You should:
   a) understand circuit diagrams, and be able to draw them;
   b) be able to set up an electric circuit from a circuit diagram;
   c) be able to connect an ammeter correctly into a circuit;
   d) be able to read the scale on an ammeter;
   e) know the differences between series and parallel circuits;
   f) know the effect of changing the number of batteries or lamps in an electric circuit;
   g) know that electric current does not 'get lost'—it is 'conserved';
   h) know what fuses are, what they are for and how they work;
   i) know why we use a water circuit as an analogy for an electric circuit;
   j) know what sort of substances are good conductors, and which are insulators.

2 You should know what each of the following is, or what each does:

electric circuit	dual-range meter
microcomputer	digital meter
integrated circuit	analogue meter
electric current	water circuit
series circuit	analogy
parallel circuit	mains supply
filament	insulator
heating effect	conductor
fuse	resistor
symbol	resistance
ammeter	rheostat
ampere (amp)	

3 These are some of the other words that have been used in this chapter. You should know what each word means:

convenient	connect
available	robust
deceptive	conclusion
component	variable
efficient	

FURTHER QUESTIONS

1 Each of the circuits shown in Fig. 2.52 shows lamps in a circuit. If the lamp in circuit (a) is 'normally bright' how bright are the lamps in each of the other circuits? Normally bright, dimmer than normal, brighter than normal or off?

2 If the circuit shown in Fig. 2.53 is connected, the lamp is almost certain to be damaged.
   a) Why? What will happen to the lamp?
   b) Explain how a fuse could be used in this circuit to prevent the lamp

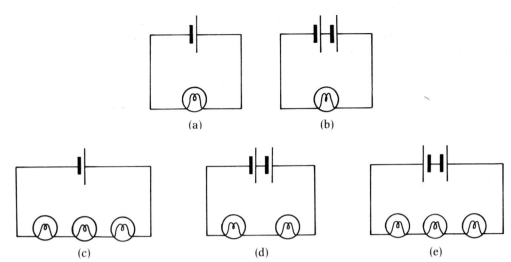

(a)

(b)

(c)

(d)

(e)

Fig. 2.52

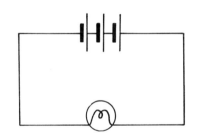

Fig. 2.53

being damaged.

c) How does a fuse work?

3 In Fig. 2.54(i) the lamp is 'normally bright'.

a) How bright, by comparison, are the lamps in the other circuits?

b) Are the lamps in each of the other circuits in series or parallel?

c) Draw circuit (iii) and include two switches, one to turn off each of the lamps.

4 a) Draw a diagram to show how you would connect three batteries to three lamps in one circuit so that each lamp is normally lit.

Fig. 2.54

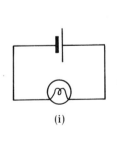

(i)

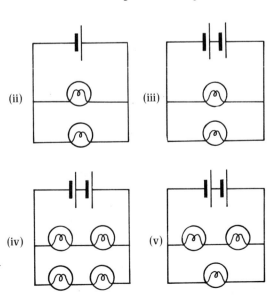

(ii)

(iii)

(iv)

(v)

b) Draw a second diagram to show how the three lamps could all be 'normally lit' from just one battery.

5 The ammeter U in Fig. 2.55 reads 0.3 A. What do the other ammeters in the circuit read?

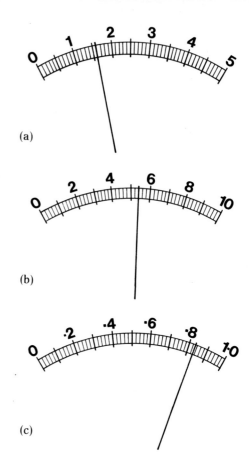

(a)

(b)

(c)

Fig. 2.57

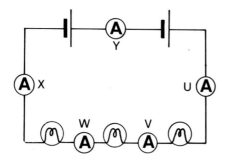

Fig. 2.55

6 In the circuits shown in Fig. 2.56, the ammeter M reads 0.3 A. Write down the readings on the various ammeters in the other circuits, choosing your answer from 0, less than 0.3 A, 0.3 A or more than 0.3 A.

7 What are the readings on the ammeter scales shown in Fig. 2.57?

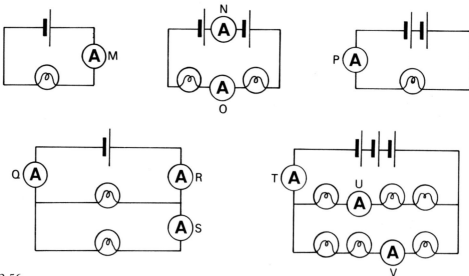

Fig. 2.56

8 Fig. 2.58 shows a water circuit. Draw an electric circuit that is similar to this water circuit.

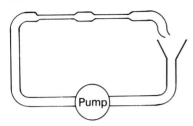

Fig. 2.58

9 a) Draw the circuit shown in Fig. 2.59(a) and include a variable resistor that would dim lamp L2 without affecting the other two lamps.
   b) A pupil drew the circuit shown in Fig. 2.59(b) in answer to the above question. What is wrong with this circuit? (There are two things wrong.)

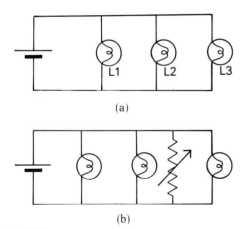

(a)

(b)

Fig. 2.59

10 In the circuit shown in Fig. 2.60, ammeter B reads 0.2 A. What do all the other ammeters read?

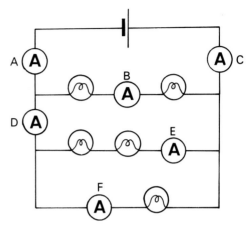

Fig. 2.60

11 Why do you think *gold* wires are used in the integrated circuit of Fig. 2.6 to connect the chip to the pins on the case?

12 Suggest two possible problems there might be in manufacturing the integrated circuit shown in Fig. 2.6.

13 Suggest two possible problems there might be in putting up the large circuit of which part is shown in Fig. 2.4.

14 Can you think of any other advantages of a digital ammeter other than that mentioned in Section 2.7?

15 Why would it be impossible to make an electric circuit without insulators?

ELECTROMAGNETISM

Fig. 3.1   All of these objects have something to do with magnets

3.1   Magnets

What have the loudspeaker, the compass, the ammeter, the tape recorder and the electric motor, all shown in Fig. 3.1, in common? Answer: they all have something to do with **magnetism**. The loudspeaker, ammeter and electric motor depend on a magnet inside in order to work at all, the compass is just a magnet that can swing round to follow the Earth's magnetic field, and the tape used by a tape recorder is covered with a very fine magnetic powder.

This chapter is mainly about **electromagnets**, which need an electric current to make them magnetic, whereas all the things shown in Fig. 3.1 involve **permanent magnets**, which are magnetic all the time.

It would be useful to know what permanent magnets do before going on to investigate electromagnets. You may well have played with magnets before, and think you know all about them, but let's look at magnets as a physicist would.

3.2 Investigating permanent magnets

Use just one bar magnet to start with to find the answers to the following questions:
1 Does your magnet attract *anything*, or only particular substances?
2 Does the magnetic force go *through* anything, like paper or wood?
3 Are all parts of the magnet equally strong or good at attracting objects? Are the two ends equally strong, for example?

Fig. 3.2 might help you with question 3; it shows a magnet that has been dipped in iron filings. Beware if you try this for yourself! It takes a long time to get the filings off the magnet again.

Fig. 3.2   Iron filings clinging to a magnet

Now use a second magnet as well as the first, and find out how they affect each other. You could either hang one magnet from a wooden or aluminium support as shown in Fig. 3.3 and bring the other one up to it, or you could put one magnet on the bench and slide the other one towards it as in Fig. 3.4.

Fig. 3.3   Do magnets attract each other?

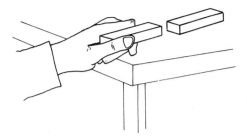

Fig. 3.4   Another way of finding out whether magnets attract each other

Why would it be wrong to use a steel rod in the apparatus illustrated in Fig. 3.3?

Do the two magnets attract each other? Do they always do the same thing?

The ends of the magnet where the force is concentrated are called the **poles** of the magnet. A word of warning! Not all magnets are long and thin, and not all magnets have their poles at the ends. The two *kinds* of poles that you have noticed are called **north poles** and **south poles**. A magnet has one of each. You will see why they have these names later.

Write a summary of what magnets do to each other by copying the following paragraph, choosing the correct words from the list at the end to fill in the gaps.

'The force from a magnet is concentrated at two _____, called the north _____ and the _____ _____. If the north _____ of one magnet is brought near the north _____ of another magnet then they _____ each other. If two south _____ are brought together they _____ each other. If the north _____ of one magnet and the south _____ of another magnet are brought together they _____ each other. We can say this more briefly: like poles _____, unlike _____ _____.'

List of possible words:
pole, end, poles, repel, attract, ignore, do nothing to.

3.3 Magnetic fields

You can find out something else interesting about magnets by laying one on its side on the bench, placing a piece of card on top of it (as shown in Fig. 3.5) and scattering some iron filings from a pepper pot onto the card. Tap the card gently once or twice. The iron filings will settle down into a pattern. Draw a diagram of the pattern.

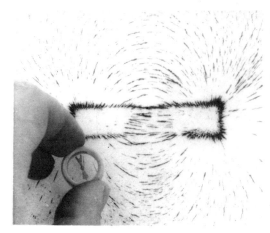

Fig. 3.6   A plotting compass shows the direction of a magnetic field

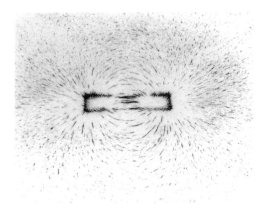

Fig. 3.5   The shape of a magnetic field can be shown using iron filings

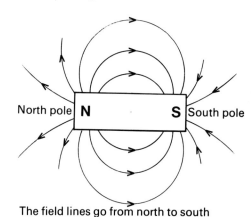

The field lines go from north to south

Fig. 3.7   The shape and direction of a magnetic field round a bar magnet

The area of magnetism round a magnet is called a **magnetic field**, and your iron filings show up what we call the *shape* of the magnetic field. Another important idea about a magnetic field is shown if you put a small compass at various points in the field. Fig. 3.6 shows such a compass being used; it is called a **plotting compass**.

A compass is just a small magnet pivoted in the centre so it can swing. The end with the arrowhead is the north pole of the little magnet. Notice how the compass points along the lines of your iron filings—along the **field lines**. Physicists say that the field lines 'go' in the direction in which your compass points—from the north pole of your big magnet to the south pole, as in Fig. 3.7. Of course, the lines are not going anywhere in the sense of moving!

On the diagram that you have drawn showing the shape of the magnetic field, add arrows to some of the field lines showing the direction in which the plotting compass points.

A magnetic field is rather more difficult to think about than a magnet. You can pick up a magnet, hold it in your hands, and show it to somebody. You cannot do this with a magnetic field. A magnetic field is an *abstract* idea.

Happiness is another abstract idea. You cannot pick it up, you cannot touch it, but you know it does exist. How do you know happiness exists? How do you know there is such a thing as a magnetic field? Write down a few more abstract ideas.

Fig. 3.8   How do you know he is happy?

3.4   The Earth's magnetic field

It is well known that there is a magnetic field round the Earth and that a compass, if it is not near another magnet, will point roughly north. This fact was first discovered by the Chinese over 2000 years ago; they are thought to be the first people to use compasses so they could navigate their ships out of sight of land without the danger of going round in circles.

The terms 'north pole' and 'south pole' come from the use of a magnet as a compass. Remember that a compass is only a magnet supported in the middle so that it can twist round. One end of the magnet was attracted towards the north and so was called the 'north-seeking pole' while the other end was attracted towards the south and so was called the 'south-seeking pole'. In time, the word 'seeking' has been dropped, leaving us with 'north pole' and 'south pole'.

The Earth is *behaving* as if there is a giant magnet inside it (see Fig. 3.9). Notice that the north pole of this imaginary magnet is at the south geographical pole. Think about that one!

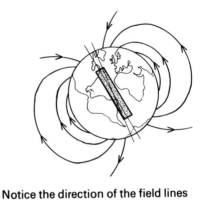

Notice the direction of the field lines

Fig. 3.9   The Earth behaves as if there is a giant magnet inside it

Of course, nobody believes there really is a magnet inside the Earth, but nobody is sure what *does* cause the magnetism.

Certainly the magnetic field does some strange things. Compasses do not point to the true north pole. At present (1982) they point about 8° west of true north in Britain, although the exact figure depends on where in Britain you are. This figure is decreasing by about 1° in 6 years. In the early nineteenth century magnetic north was as much as 24° west of true north, while in the seventeenth century magnetic north was about 10° *east* of true north.

Even more surprising, there is evidence that at several periods in the past, long before man inhabited this planet, magnetic north was in the Antarctic! Scientists have discovered that the field has 'flipped over' 17 times in the last 4 million years, the last change being nearly $\frac{3}{4}$ million years ago.

Can you find out what this evidence is? There certainly were no men around with compasses! (The clue lies in the rocks on the floors of the oceans.)

33

3.5 Making an electromagnet

This is quite easy to do. Use a 'C' shaped piece of iron such as is shown in Fig. 3.10. First check whether your iron is magnetic by itself. Will it pick up any iron or steel?

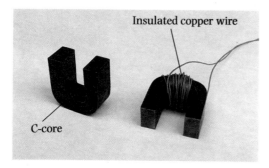

Fig. 3.10 Making an electromagnet

Fig. 3.12 A large electromagnet in use in a scrapyard

Wind about 40 to 50 turns of thin, insulated wire round your C-core, as in the photograph, and connect the bare ends to a suitable low voltage (about 4 volts) electric power supply. Switch on the electricity. Is your iron magnetic? Is it very strong? Use your electromagnet to attract another iron C-core, as Mike and Paul are doing in Fig. 3.11 to feel how strong the magnetic forces can be.

To make a stronger electromagnet you could use a larger electric current, but there is a disadvantage in using a large current. Can you think what it is?

Large electromagnets, such as the one in Fig. 3.12, are used for lifting steel objects and sorting out scrap iron, for example.

You could next investigate the shape and direction of the magnetic field round your electromagnet, using card, iron filings and a plotting compass as in Fig. 3.13. Sketch the field shape and direction in your notebook.

Now that you know how to make an electromagnet, there are two *kinds* of questions you could next try to answer. You could ask questions like 'How does it work?' or 'Why does the iron become magnetic?' or 'Do we need to *coil* the wire to make the iron magnetic?'. These are the sort of questions a **physicist** might ask. Or you could ask 'How can we use

Fig. 3.11 How strong is *your* electromagnet?

Pepper pot full of iron filings

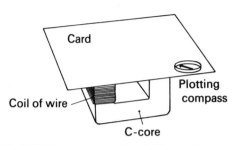

Card

Coil of wire

Plotting compass

C-core

Fig. 3.13   Investigating the field round an electromagnet

Fig. 3.14   How do you arrange this apparatus to make a buzzer? Do you need anything else?

it?' or 'How can we design an electromagnet that is strong enough to pick up a car?' This is the sort of question that an **engineer** tries to answer. Of course, an engineer is often interested in *why* something works, but, to quote Professor Eric Laithwaite, 'You don't need to know *how* something works in order to make use of it.' The engineer responsible for the design of the locomotive *Lion* in Fig. 1.4 knew nothing about the physics of changing heat energy to kinetic energy, but the locomotive was a successful piece of engineering in its time.

3.6   Bells and buzzers

Try being an engineer for a while. There are lots of ways of using electromagnets: electric buzzers and bells are two ways. To make a model of a buzzer, clamp the middle of a strip of steel (an old hacksaw blade will do) to a block of wood on the bench as in Fig. 3.14.

You need **alternating current** for your buzzer. Alternating current flows round the circuit first one way, then the other, usually changing its direction many times a second. In Britain, the mains supply gives out alternating current which completes a 'forwards and back-

wards' sequence in 1/50th second, or 50 'cycles' in a second.

Connect your electromagnet to an alternating current supply (about 4 volts). Where are you going to put your electromagnet so that the steel buzzes? See if you can carry on from here to make a really effective buzzer.

Answer the following questions:
1 Why do you think alternating current is used for a buzzer?
2 Is there a 'best place' to clamp the steel blade?
3 How did you make your buzzer give a *loud* noise?

Since a buzzer uses alternating current, it cannot be supplied with electricity from a battery, which gives **direct current**. A bell which runs off a battery is in many ways similar to a buzzer, but it has an extra part to switch the current to the electromagnet on and off repeatedly so that the steel blade is repeatedly pulled towards and then springs away from the electromagnet. This extra part is called a 'make-and-break device'.

Try to make a bell to work off direct current using the same equipment as you used for a buzzer. Try to design a make-and-break device. If you are really stuck Fig. 3.15 over the page might help you, but it is better if you try to think of your own design.

Draw your design in your notebook (when it works!). Briefly explain how your bell works.

Fig. 3.15   The make-and-break part of a model bell. How does it work?

Fig. 3.16 shows the inside of a commercially produced bell. (Do not assume it is necessarily better than your design!) Try to find the make-and-break device on this bell.

Fig. 3.16   Inside a real bell

3.7   Relays (or electromagnetic switches)

The same apparatus with which you made a buzzer and a bell can be used to make another useful device. Electrical engineers often need to be able to switch on a circuit which carries a *lot* of current by using another electric circuit which carries a comparatively small current. To

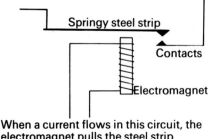

When a current flows in this circuit, the electromagnet pulls the steel strip towards it, so closing the contacts of the other circuit

Fig. 3.17   The outline of a simple relay

do this, they use an electromagnetic switch, or **relay**. The outline of the idea is shown in Fig. 3.17.

Relays are used, for example, to switch on the current to the starter motor of a car, for switching currents in the national grid and for switching telephone calls in telephone exchanges.

Fig. 3.18 shows a model relay built with the apparatus you have been using. Try to use the photograph to build a model relay for yourself. Work out what each part is there for, and what it is doing. Try to think of ways of improving the design.

Fig. 3.18   Part of a simple model relay. Can you improve on this design?

Make a diagram of your design in your notebook. Write a few words explaining how it works.

How could you modify the design so that a circuit with a lamp is switched *off* when the electromagnet is switched *on*?

The photograph in Fig. 3.19 shows a close-up view of a real relay; this is a miniature one such as is found in

Fig. 3.19 A miniature relay. Try to decide what each part is for

Fig. 3.20 Most of your telephone calls are still switched by relays. Inside a telephone exchange

When you made your electromagnet, you used an iron core and a coil of wire. Why did you get any magnetism? Is it something to do with the iron, or the wire, or the electric current, or what? To sort out an answer to this problem, you must take your electromagnet apart step by step.

Start by sliding the coil off the core. Put your coil on the bench near some iron filings and a plotting compass as in Fig. 3.21. Switch on the current. Is there any magnetism without the iron core there? Is there *much* magnetism? Can you suggest why an electromagnet has an iron core?

electronic circuits. Fig. 3.20 shows relays in a telephone exchange. Such telephone exchanges are gradually to be replaced with all-electronic exchanges.

3.8 Magnetic fields and electric currents

In this section you are going to stop being an engineer for a while and become a physicist again to look at electromagnets in more detail.

Fig. 3.21 Will this coil be magnetic if an electric current passes through it?

37

What is the shape of the magnetic field near a coil of wire? Investigate this using the apparatus in Fig. 3.22. Sketch the shape of the field in your book. Does it make any difference if the coil is compact [Fig. 3.22(b)] or spread out [Fig. 3.22(c)]?

Does the wire have to be in a coil for there to be a magnetic field? Will an electric current going along a single length of wire make a magnetic field? Fig. 3.23 should suggest to you how you might carry out an investigation to answer this question.

Now write a *summary* of what you have learned in this section by copying out the following paragraph, filling in the gaps using words and phrases from the lists at the end. Fill in gap A with a word from list A, gap B with a phrase from list B, and so on.

'In an electromagnet, an iron core is
    A   , since without it there   B
    magnetic field. With an electric current going along a single length of wire we can obtain   C   . If we wind the wire into a coil we   D   .'

List A
useful
essential
useless

Fig. 3.22   Investigating the magnetic field round a coil of wire

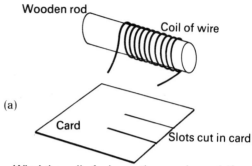

(a)

Wind the coil of wire on the wooden rod, then slide it off into the slots in the card

(b)

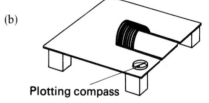

(c)

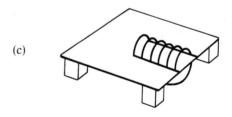

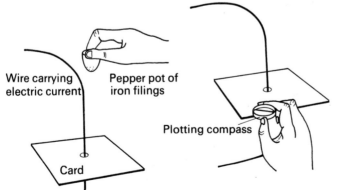

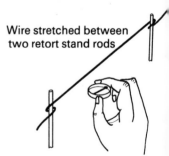

Fig. 3.23   Investigating the field round a wire carrying an electric current

38

List B
would be no
would only be a weak
is a strong enough

List C
a magnetic field of no regular shape
no magnetic field
a circular shaped field going round the wire
a square shaped field

List D
still get no magnetic field
get a weaker field
get a stronger field spiralling round the coil
get a stronger field of similar shape to a bar magnet's field

3.9 The 'catapult' effect

Earlier in this chapter you saw that there is a force between two magnets that are close together. Suppose you replace one of the magnets with a wire through which there is flowing an electric current? There is a magnetic field round the wire. Will there be any sort of force between the wire and the magnet? There are at least two ways in which you could try to find out.

The first way is illustrated in Fig. 3.24. An electric current flows along a length of aluminium foil. The foil goes between the poles of a horseshoe-shaped magnet.

Set up this apparatus and switch on the current. What happens when the current is switched on? Are there any forces anywhere?

Does it make any difference if the current goes the other way through the aluminium foil?

Does it make any difference if the magnet is turned round so that the field is going the other way?

A second way of investigating the problem is shown in Fig. 3.25. Two thick pieces of copper wire are attached to the low voltage terminals of a power supply, to act as 'rails'. The ends are turned up as shown to act as 'buffers'. A loose piece of wire is laid across these rails so that it can slide along them. When the current is switched on it will go along this loose piece of wire.

Fig. 3.25   What happens to the loose piece of wire when a current is flowing?

Fig. 3.24   What happens when a current passes along the aluminium foil?

Hold a horseshoe magnet round the loose wire. (You can make a horseshoe magnet from two slab magnets and an iron 'yoke' as shown. Make sure opposite poles of the magnet face inwards. The poles of these magnets are on the large faces.) Switch on the current.

Does anything happen to the loose piece of wire when the current is switched on?

Does anything different happen if the magnet is turned over so that the field runs the other way?

In both experiments notice that the direction of the electric current along the wire is at right angles to the direction of the magnetic field (Fig. 3.26). In which direction is the force on the wire—in the same direction as the current, along the magnetic field, or what?

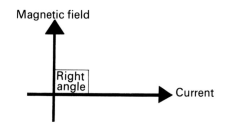

Magnetic field

Right angle

Current

Fig. 3.26   The magnetic field is at right angles to the direction of the current. Which way does the wire move?

This experiment is sometimes called the electromagnetic **catapult effect**. Can you see why?

Fig. 3.27   Why is this called the catapult field?

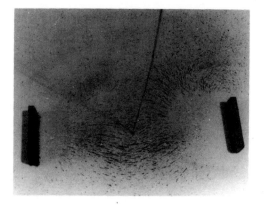

Fig. 3.27 might help you answer this question. It is a photograph of iron filings being used to show up the magnetic field lines near the wire and slab magnets in the catapult experiment. Look at the shape of the field.

3.10   The moving-coil ammeter

You are now going to be an engineer again to make use of the catapult effect that you have just investigated. You have probably already used a moving-coil ammeter in the work in Chapter 2, for measuring electric currents. You can now find out how it works.

Fig. 3.28 shows how the idea of an ammeter can be built up from the catapult effect. The wire in diagram (a) has an electric current flowing through it. Since it is going through a magnetic field there will be a force pushing the wire. This force will be at right angles to the field and to the direction of the current. Let us suppose that it is pushed *down*. If the wire is bent to a loop [diagram (b)] then one side will be pushed up while the other side is pushed down. (Why?) If this loop is mounted on an axle [diagram (c)] then the loop will rotate until one half of the loop is as high as it can go, and the other half is as low as it can go [diagram (d)].

If this were all you did, then the loop would always rotate until it was vertical, no matter how much current was flowing round the loop. To overcome this, a pair of coil springs are added to the axle as in diagram (e). The more current there is in the loop, the more force there is, the more the springs can be twisted and the more the loop of wire turns. The springs will also send the loop back to horizontal when the current is switched off.

The loop of wire can be wound into several loops, or a coil, to increase the force [diagram (f)]. The coil springs can be used to get the current into and out of the coil of wire [diagram (g)]. A pointer

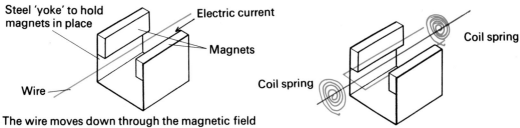

Steel 'yoke' to hold magnets in place

Electric current

Magnets

Wire

The wire moves down through the magnetic field

(a) A long straight wire in a magnetic field

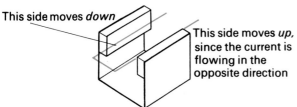

This side moves *down*

This side moves *up*, since the current is flowing in the opposite direction

(b) The wire is bent into a loop

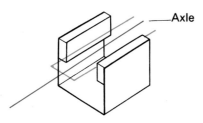

Axle

(c) The loop is mounted on an axle so that it can rotate

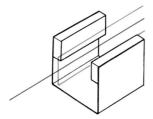

(d) An electric current flowing in the loop would make it rotate until it was vertical

Fig. 3.28   The idea behind the moving coil ammeter

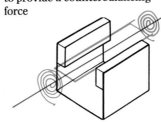

Coil spring

Coil spring

(e) Add coil springs to the axle to provide a counterbalancing force

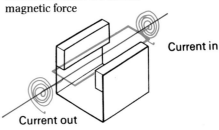

(f) Wind the loop into several turns to increase the electro-magnetic force

Current in

Current out

(g) Use the coil springs to pass the current into and out of the turns of wire

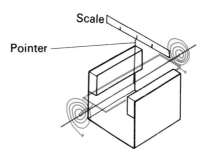

Scale

Pointer

(h) Add a pointer and a scale

and a scale [diagram (h)] complete the idea.

Now, can you make a model ammeter based on these ideas? Fig. 3.29 shows an example of a completed model, while Fig. 3.30 shows an 'exploded' view so that you can see how the parts fit together.

Start by wrapping about 10 turns of thin, insulated wire round a wooden 'former'. Leave at least $\frac{1}{4}$ metre of loose wire at each end. You may need some Sellotape to help keep the wire in place. Use some of each of the two ends of the wire to make two *loose* spiral springs of about 4 turns. Fix the coil onto the wooden base using split pins and an aluminium axle as shown, and anchor each end of the wire under two rivets   41

Fig. 3.29　A model moving coil meter based on the ideas in Fig. 3.28

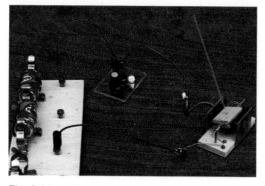

Fig. 3.31　Using the simple model ammeter

as shown. Place the whole assembly between two slab (or magnadur) magnets mounted on an iron yoke with opposite poles facing as in the diagram. Add a straw pointer.

Connect your model into a simple circuit with a power supply and a variable resistor as in Fig. 3.31. Switch on the current. What happens to your ammeter when you switch on the current?

Does it make any difference if the current passes through your meter the other way? (Reverse the connections to the power supply.)

What happens to your meter if you *increase* the current passing through it by adjusting the variable resistor?

The loose spiral springs on the ammeter are important. Write down two separate reasons for their being there.

The *sensitivity* of an ammeter is the amount by which the tip of the pointer moves for every unit of current passing through the meter. What ways can you think of for making your ammeter more sensitive? (There are four possible ways.)

Fig. 3.30　An exploded view of the moving coil meter. Can you make one?

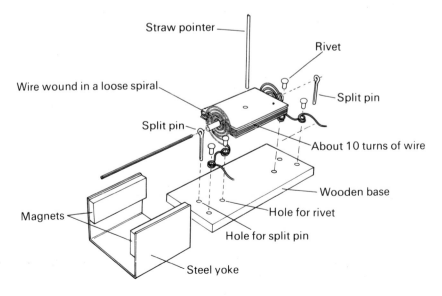

Straw pointer

Rivet

Wire wound in a loose spiral

Split pin

Split pin

About 10 turns of wire

Wooden base

Magnets

Hole for rivet

Hole for split pin

Steel yoke

42

Have a look inside a real moving-coil ammeter if you can, or look at Fig. 3.32. Can you see the magnets, the coil, the spiral springs and the pointer?

Write down a list of all the ways in which the real ammeter is similar to your model, and all the ways in which it is different.

Fig. 3.32   The movement of a real ammeter. Can you identify the parts?

3.11   The electric motor

There are many kinds of electric motor; the simple, direct-current motor that you are going to make uses the same basic ideas as the ammeter; you can use the same parts to build a motor as you did to build an ammeter.

Like the ammeter, the motor has a coil of wire that turns on an axle. Since the motor must keep turning, there are no spiral springs to stop it doing so. But there are two problems.

The first problem is that the current must be taken to and from the motor without the turning of the motor twisting up the wires supplying the current. The second problem is illustrated in Fig. 3.33 (which is similar to Fig. 3.28). The loop of wire starts to turn, with one side going up and the other side going down, in exactly the same way as was explained for the

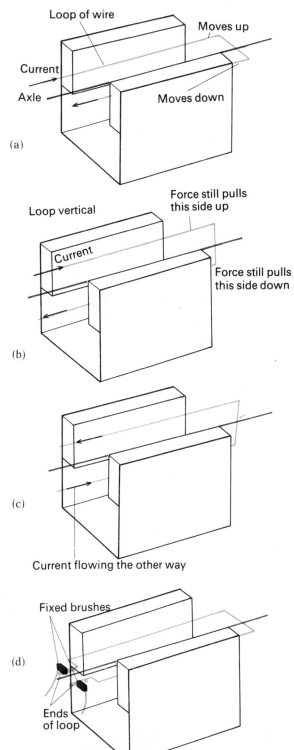

Fig. 3.33   The idea behind the simple electric motor

43

ammeter in the last section. When the loop becomes vertical, the side that was going up will still have a force on it pushing it up, although of course it cannot actually move up any further. But we now want this side to start moving down [Fig. 3.33(c)]. To do this, we must make the current flow round the loop of wire in the *opposite* direction.

You can solve both these problems by finishing the loop of wire in the way shown in Fig. 3.33(d). Two fixed carbon **brushes** push against the bare ends of the wire to get the current into and out of the motor without twisting any wires.

Fig. 3.34 How the brushes and commutator work

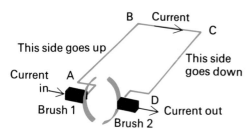

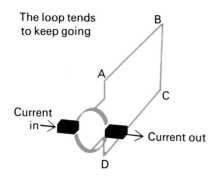

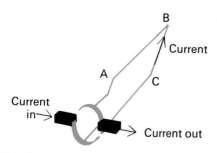

Side AB is now going down because the current is flowing the opposite way in this side to the way it was flowing in the first diagram

Fig. 3.34 explains in detail how the brush and **commutator** arrangement makes the motor turn in the same direction all the time. In the first diagram current is going in through brush 1 to the side AB of the loop. When the loop reaches the vertical position it tends to keep going until brush 1 rubs against the part of the commutator leading to side CD, so the current now goes the other way round the loop. This is what we wanted. The loop will keep turning in the same direction.

3.12 Making a model motor

A drawing of the motor is shown in Fig. 3.35, while Fig. 3.36 shows what the finished motor should look like. Using these illustrations try to make a model motor for yourself.

After you have made your motor, connect it to a power supply (about 6 volts). It will probably need a push to start it. Try to think of and build one or two improvements to your motor.

Now answer these questions:
1 What happens to your motor if you connect the power supply the other way, so that the current flows in the opposite direction?
2 Alternating current flows backwards then forwards many times a second. What do you think would happen if

Fig. 3.36 A finished model motor

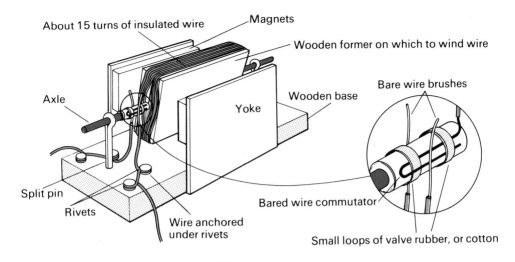

About 15 turns of insulated wire

Magnets

Wooden former on which to wind wire

Bare wire brushes

Axle

Wooden base

Yoke

Split pin

Rivets

Wire anchored under rivets

Bared wire commutator

Small loops of valve rubber, or cotton

Fig. 3.35   The model motor shown in Fig. 3.36

Fig. 3.37   Close up of brushes and commutator

Fig. 3.38   This model motor uses an electromagnet rather than a permanent magnet. The brushes and commutator are at the bottom and not visible

you tried to use alternating current with your motor?

3 Some motors use electromagnets instead of permanent magnets. Fig. 3.38 shows a model of such a motor. Do you think this motor can be used with alternating current? Explain your answer.

4 Fig. 3.38 shows another difference between your model motor and a real motor—the real motors have more than one coil, and a commutator with correspondingly more segments. Can you think of a reason for this?

You will have noticed that there is a lot of sparking with your motor, and that the wire brushes are easily burnt or **oxidized**.

45

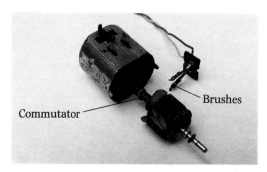

Fig. 3.39   The parts of a cheap electric motor. A hole has been worn in one of the copper brushes

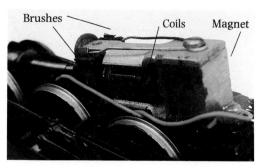

Fig. 3.40   A motor used in a model railway locomotive

Fig. 3.39 shows the parts of a cheap electric motor with copper brushes. You can see that they are beginning to corrode away and there is a black layer of copper oxide which makes it difficult for the electricity to flow into the commutator.

The next photograph shows a more expensive motor with carbon brushes which are pushed against the commutator with a spring. Why do you think carbon brushes are better? (What is made when carbon is oxidized in the heat of the sparks?)

Not all motors work in the same way as your model. Fig. 3.41 shows a gramophone motor. However hard you look, you will not find any brushes or commutator. There are neither, so there is no sparking either. The motor is one sort of **induction** motor, and works in a totally different way to your model. Many big industrial motors are induction motors. The motors which drive the lathes and milling machines in your school workshops are probably induction motors. Why do you think a motor that does not spark is a good thing for a record player?

Fig. 3.41   A motor from a record player. There are no brushes or commutator

---

SUMMARY

Now that you have finished this chapter on electromagnetism, there are a number of things that you should know and be able to do.

1 You should:

 a) know that magnets have a north and a south pole, and that unlike poles attract, like poles repel;

 b) know how to show up the shape and direction of magnetic field lines using iron filings and a compass;

 c) know various common shapes of

magnetic fields;
d) be able to make an electromagnet, and be able to use it to make a bell, a buzzer and a relay;
e) be able to explain how a bell, buzzer and relay work;
f) have had some experience at trying to design things;
g) know how to make use of the catapult effect to make an ammeter and a motor;
h) be able to explain how an ammeter works;
i) know how to change the sensitivity of an ammeter;
j) be able to explain how a motor works;
k) have some idea of what an engineer does.

2 You should know what each of the following is, or what each does:

electromagnet	alternating
permanent magnet	current
north pole	direct current
south pole	relay
magnetic field	catapult effect
plotting compass	sensitivity
field line	commutator
induction motor	brush

3 These are some of the other words that have been used in this chapter. You should know what each word means:

attract	regular
repel	spiral
abstract	rotate
advantage	vertical
disadvantage	horizontal
summary	oxidize

_____FURTHER QUESTIONS_____

1 The diagrams in Fig. 3.42 show various magnetic field patterns formed by iron filings. Write down what you think caused each pattern (e.g. one magnet, two magnets attracting, etc.).

Fig. 3.42

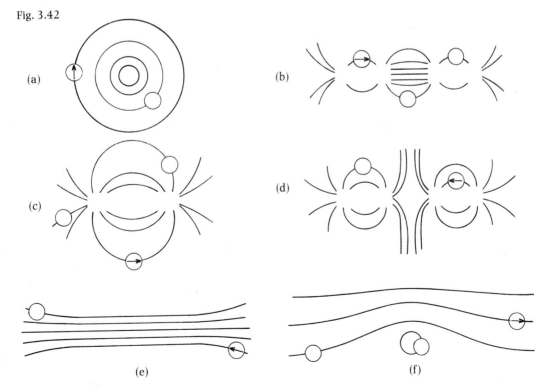

(a)

(b)

(c)

(d)

(e)

(f)

2 Each of the diagrams in Fig. 3.42 have on them a number of circles representing plotting compasses. Some of the needles on the compasses have been shown. Copy the diagrams and draw in the remaining needles.

3 In trying to design a bell, a pupil produced the design shown in Fig. 3.43. What will happen when the electric current is switched on? Can you think of any use for this device as it stands?

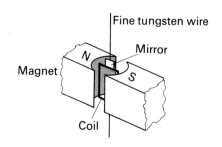

Fig. 3.44

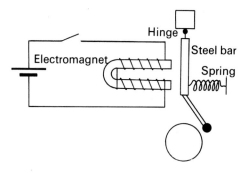

Fig. 3.43

4 The make-and-break device (or 'contact breaker') for a bell is often coated with a metal like platinum. Why?

5 Design an electric circuit, using a relay, which rings a bell if the door of a room is opened.

6 Modify the design you produced for the last question so that the bell keeps ringing even if the door is closed again.

7 a) Some very sensitive ammeters do not have spiral springs; the coil is hung between two pieces of fine tungsten wire as in Fig. 3.44. How can such meters work without a spiral spring?

   b) The same ammeters do not have a pointer; there is a small mirror on the coil which turns with the coil. A beam of light is reflected off the coil on to a screen with a scale. What do you think is the advantage of this system compared to the usual pointer?

8 Explain in your own words how the brush and commutator arrangement allows a motor to keep turning in the same direction.

9 A friend of yours makes a model electric motor, finds it does not work and asks you to help. What would you check to find out why the motor was not working?

10 Write a short essay explaining whether you would rather be an engineer, a scientist, or neither. Give some examples of the sort of work you think engineers and scientists do to help your explanation.

4

TIME AND MOVEMENT
TIME AND MOVEMENT

TIME AND MOVEMENT

Fig. 4.1 The Sun—man's earliest clock

4.1 Introduction

How do you tell the time? What a silly question you might think! You use a clock (or a watch). Suppose the same question had been asked 2000 years ago, could the same answer have been given? Have there always been such things as clocks? It is worth spending a little time thinking about how clocks tell the time for you.

A day was the most obvious and simple unit of time for primitive man. The sun regularly rose in the east, travelled across the sky and set in the west. But the day is quite a *long* time, and man needed to divide the day into smaller intervals. Many primitive people told the time by the position of the sun in the sky and the idea of pushing a stick in the ground and looking at the position of the shadow soon followed (Fig. 4.2). The Babylonians and the Egyptians certainly used shadow clocks.

The idea of dividing the day into 12 equal parts (hours) goes back to the earliest civilizations. Since the length of

49

Fig. 4.2 A simple shadow clock

Fig. 4.3 A sundial

Fig. 4.4 A sundial on the side of a house. The date on the sundial is 1681. What was the time when the photograph was taken?

the day varied with the time of the year, the length of these early hours varied too with the time of the year—short hours in winter and long hours in summer. In Europe, this system lasted until the middle ages, but it went on until the nineteenth century in Japan.

Dividing up the night was a later idea. Armies probably wanted to time things at night as well as during the day. Why do you think this was? The night was also divided into 12 hours, which gave 24 for the whole day.

(Notice our language has the same word—'day'—meaning both 'the time for which it is light' and '24 hours'. Most languages are the same—one word means both things. Have you any idea why?)

Look at the sundial in Fig. 4.3 (a modern 'shadow clock'). The 12 o'clock position is on the north side. Why? Also explain why 6 o'clock in the morning is on the west side and 6 o'clock in the evening is on the east side.

What disadvantages are there in using a sundial?

Shadows cast by the sun can also be used to tell the time of the year. How can this be done? What would you have to measure? Some people think that Stonehenge (Fig. 4.5) is a giant calendar that was used for telling the time of the year. Why do you think it was important for primitive people to be able to tell what time of year it was?

4.2 Different sorts of clocks

Fig. 4.6 shows a number of different arrangements of apparatus. Set up these arrangements for yourself. Could any of them be used as a simple clock? Do you think any of them would make a *good*

Fig. 4.5 Stonehenge. Was this a giant calendar?

(a) Sand timer

(b) Water clock

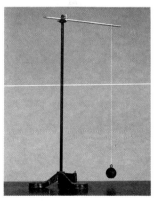

(c) Candle

(e) Simple pendulum

(d) Spiral spring with weight

Fig. 4.6 Could you use any of this equipment as a 'clock'? Would they be very good clocks?

clock? Can you think of any way of improving these simple clocks? What is obviously missing from these 'clocks' compared to the clocks that you are used to every day? (See Fig. 4.7.) Do any of these simple clocks remind you of any sort of clock or timer that you have seen outside the lab?

Fig. 4.7   An everyday clock

Fig. 4.8   Cast of an Egyptian water clock

4.3   The pendulum clock

Until recently, most clocks were controlled (or *regulated*) by something like a **pendulum**, which swung backwards and forwards in a regular way, or by a spring, which twisted backwards and forwards. (Many modern clocks and watches are controlled by a crystal which vibrates and controls the oscillations of electrons.)

The pendulum only controls the speed at which the clock hands move. The hands are actually moved by a **mainspring** or falling weights. Fig. 4.9 shows the way in which a pendulum controls the speed of a clock.

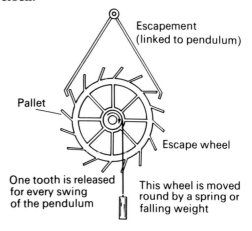

Fig. 4.9   How a pendulum controls a clock

But what is it about a pendulum that makes it good for controlling a clock? The following experiment will help you to find out. Fig. 4.10 shows Fiona using one possible arrangement. Pull the mass back 5 centimetres and then use a stopclock to time how long it takes to complete 10 full swings (forwards and back). Why is this better than timing just one swing? To do this accurately, it is best to start and finish timing the pendulum as it goes through the midpoint of the swing. If you use the arrangement in Fig. 4.10 then stand or sit so you can line up the two retort stands with your eye as Fiona is doing in the photograph. The pendulum is in the middle of its swing when it is lined up with the two rods. Release the pendulum and count '2, 1, 0, 1, 2, 3, . . .' as the pendulum passes the stands in the same direction each time, starting the stopclock as you say '0'. Stop the clock on '10'. Write down how long it takes for 10 swings.

Do you think it is wise to repeat the experiment and take the average of the two results? Do so if you think it is sensible.

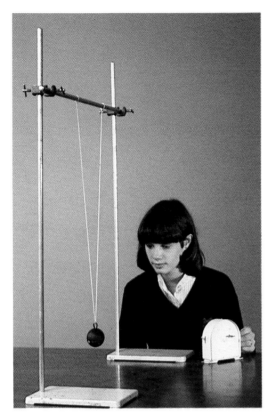

Fig. 4.10 Fiona timing a simple pendulum. Notice the way of supporting the bob, and where Fiona is sitting

Now do the experiment again, but this time pull the $\frac{1}{2}$ kilogram mass back 10 cm to start the pendulum. How long does it take for ten swings this time? Then try again with the pendulum starting 15 cm from the centre of the swing.

Fig. 4.11 Huygen's original clock

What do you notice about all the times you have measured? Can you see why a pendulum is so useful for controlling a clock?

It was Galileo who first investigated a pendulum in the way you have just done. Although he thought of how he could use a pendulum to control a clock, he died before he was able to make a pendulum clock. Christian Huygens made the first pendulum clock in 1657.

4.4 Fast and slow

Look at the running hare in Fig. 4.12. There are a few simple ways to describe how it is running. For example, you could say it is running *fast*. But fast compared to what? Certainly, fast compared to the tortoise in Fig. 4.13, but the hare will surely be going slowly compared to the cheetah in the next picture. It all depends on what you compare the hare with. So physicists need a more precise way of describing how the hare is moving—they measure the *speed* of the hare.

The speed of the hare is *how far* the hare goes every second. The hare in the picture was probably going about 8 metres every second, so its speed is 8 metres per second, which we usually write as 8 m/s. The tortoise was only going at a speed of $\frac{1}{20}$ m/s (or 5 cm/s) while a cheetah can run at 40 m/s. If it were running down a motorway it would be breaking the speed limit.

Sometimes we measure the speed as how far something moves in one minute, or one hour, rather than one second. A car's speedometer tells you how far the car moves in one hour. So a better definition of what is meant by speed is 'speed is the distance travelled in one unit of time'. One unit of time might be 1 second, or 1 minute, 1 hour or even 1 day. We usually measure speed in m/s or cm/s in the laboratory, while km/hour or even miles/hour are more common outside the laboratory for cars, trains or aeroplanes.

53

Fig. 4.12   A running hare

Fig. 4.13   A walking tortoise

4.5   Measuring speed

How could you measure the speed at which you walk? You need to know how far you go in one second. But to walk for just one second and then stop again is a little difficult and would certainly lead to an inaccurate result. Why? It is much better to measure the time it takes to walk a longer distance, such as the length of your laboratory, and then calculate how far you go in each second.

For example, if you walk 8 metres in 4 seconds, then you would go 2 metres in every second; your speed would be 2 m/s.

Generally, you calculate your speed by dividing the *distance* you walk by the *time* it takes you:

$$\text{speed} = \frac{\text{distance travelled}}{\text{time taken}}$$

Using a metre rule to measure how far you walk, and a stopclock to measure the time you take, find out how fast you walk.

4.6   Problems with measuring time

Suppose, when you find out how fast you walk, you are not quite sure that you have measured the speed correctly. You want to check your measurements. You can get out the metre rule again and measure the distance you walked (such as the length of your lab) as many times as you like until you are satisfied with the result. But can you measure the time again with the stopclock? Only if you walk down the lab again. But this is a different experiment—it is extremely unlikely that you will walk at exactly the same speed each time you try. You have only *one* chance to measure the time, unless you can think of a way of having a *permanent record* of the experiment. Can you think of any way of doing this?

There is another problem. Ask three or four of your friends to time how long it takes you to walk the length of your lab. Do they all agree with each other? They

Fig. 4.14   A running cheetah

will probably disagree by at least $\frac{1}{2}$ second. You may think that this is not a very large disagreement, and that you need not worry about it, but the time you take to walk down the lab is probably not very long either. The disagreement among your friends, *as a fraction of the total time,* might be quite large.

This problem is even worse if the time to be measured is shorter. Ask some of your friends to time how long it takes you to jump from a stool to the floor, like Jillian in the photograph. Is it reasonable to do this with a stopclock?

Fig. 4.15   How long does Jillian take to jump off the stool? Could you time it with a stopwatch?

4.7   Timing with a cine camera

One possible way, which may have occurred to you, of overcoming the problems in the last section is to use a cine camera. A **cine camera** takes lots of photographs one after the other; Fig. 4.16 shows a short section of cine film of the cheetah which was illustrated in Fig. 4.14. You can see how much the cheetah has moved between each 'shot'. (Can you decide which of these frames was actually used for Fig. 4.14?)

The time between each **frame** of a cine film is generally about $\frac{1}{25}$th of a second, although it will be much less with a special 'high-speed' camera. So you could use cine film to examine something that happens quickly. A cine film of Jillian jumping from the stool is shown in Fig. 4.17. (Fig. 4.15 was one frame of this

Fig. 4.16   A sequence from a cine film showing a running cheetah

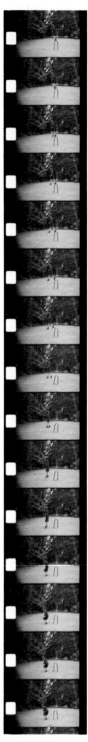

Fig. 4.17   A sequence from a cine film showing Jillian jumping from a stool   55

film—which one?) If the cine camera took one picture every $\frac{1}{25}$th of a second, how long did Jillian take to jump from the stool to the ground?

The obvious disadvantage of cine film is the expense, and the fact that the results are not available at once—the film has to be processed, which probably means sending it away.

4.8 Stroboscopic photography

There is another technique that physicists use to help them see the way in which things are moving which also involves photography, but this time with an ordinary 'still' camera. If you take a photograph with the shutter of a camera open for a fairly long time, and anything in the photograph moves in that time, that thing will be blurred. This is what has happened in Fig. 4.18. The shutter of the camera was open for about 3 seconds, and in this time Paul walked across the back of the lab. You can see from the photograph that something was moving, but the photograph tells you nothing about the details of this movement.

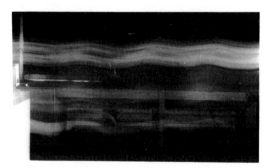

Fig. 4.18 Something moved across the back of the lab. But with what speed?

In the next photograph, Paul was illuminated with a *flashing* light, so he only shows up in the photograph at those places where he happened to be when the light flashed on. This photograph shows the details of the way Paul was moving. The light was flashing regularly. Was

Fig. 4.19 A strobe photograph of Paul walking across the back of the lab. Paul was illuminated twice every second

Paul moving at a *steady* speed, or was his speed changing? How can you tell?

The light was flashing twice every second. What other information do you need to work out *how fast* Paul was moving?

The special flashing lamp that was used is shown in Fig. 4.20. It is called a **stroboscope**. This technique of recording the way in which something moves is called **stroboscopic photography**. Fig. 4.21 is a stroboscopic photograph of a squash player hitting a ball. The stroboscope was flashing many times a second to take this photograph. At what point was the squash racket moving fastest?

A stroboscopic photograph still has to be developed, although it is possible to do this on the spot in the lab. In many cases, however, it is possible to make a

Fig. 4.20 The stroboscope used to illuminate Paul

Fig. 4.21   A squash player illuminated with stroboscopic light

permanent record of the way something moves using the simple device shown in Fig. 4.22, which will measure time intervals of $\frac{1}{50}$ second.

4.9   The ticker-tape timer

The device in Fig. 4.22 is called a **ticker-tape timer**. There are several different varieties, but all of them have a small hammer which vibrates up and down by being attracted to an electromagnet 50 times a second. (Have you ever made anything similar?) Underneath the hammer is a small disc of carbon paper, face down. Underneath this is a piece of paper tape which is attached to the moving object. As the object moves, it pulls the paper tape through the timer and it makes a dot on the paper every $\frac{1}{50}$ second as can be seen in the photo-

Fig. 4.22   A ticker-tape timer

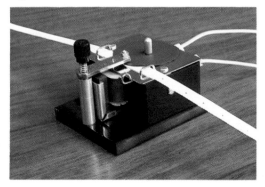

Fig. 4.23   Paul pulling tape through a ticker-tape timer

graph. The carbon paper rotates so that a hole is not quickly worn in one place.

If the tape is moving fast, will the dots be further apart or closer together than when the tape is moving slowly?

Use the ticker-tape timer to make a record of yourself walking across your lab. Use about 2 metres of tape, thread it through the timer, switch it on and walk away from the timer, pulling the tape with you. Try to change your speed while you are walking.

Rather than just *looking* at your tape when you have finished, you can get a better picture of the way you moved by making a chart like the one in Fig. 4.24. To do this, cut off and throw away the first bit of your tape where there were no dots, then count ten spaces and cut off this next bit of tape. The diagram in Fig. 4.25 should make this clear. If your timer makes 50 dots in 1 second, how long does it take to make the 10 dots worth that you have just cut off? Why do you think we do not usually cut up the tape at every dot?

57

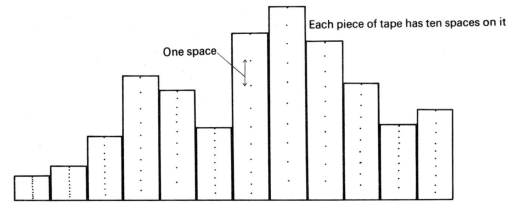

One space

Each piece of tape has ten spaces on it

Fig. 4.24   A ticker-tape chart

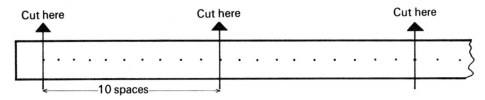

Cut here   Cut here   Cut here

←————10 spaces————→

Fig. 4.25   Cutting up the tape

Paste your piece of tape on the left side of your sheet of paper (it is obviously better to use sticky tape) and then count the next ten spaces and cut off the next piece of tape. Stick this beside the first. Continue to do this for all your tape until you have made a chart like the one in Fig. 4.24.

Mark on your chart where you were going *fastest* and where you were going *slowest*. Also mark where you were getting faster (**accelerating**) and where you were getting slower (**decelerating** or retarding).

4.10   Measuring speed from a ticker-tape chart

Look at your shortest piece of tape, where you were going slowest. Use a ruler to measure how far you went in the $\frac{1}{5}$ second that it took for this piece of tape to go through the timer. Your speed is how far you would go in 1 second, which is obviously 5 times further than how far you go in $\frac{1}{5}$ second. So you can work out your speed by multiplying the length of your tape by 5 to find out how far you would go in 1 second. Fig. 4.26 should make this clear.

Work out the speed shown by your shortest piece of tape in this way. Then work out your fastest speed.

Strictly speaking, you are working out the *average* speed shown by each of these two pieces of tape. Why are these average speeds?

4.11   Acceleration, or getting faster

When you made a tape chart showing how you moved across the room, you probably changed your speed. You might have got faster, or *accelerated*, or you might have slowed down, or *decelerated*. When Jillian jumped off the stool earlier in this chapter, she got faster as she got nearer the ground—she accelerated. Fig. 4.27 shows a strobe photograph of Jillian jumping off a stool. The strobe light was flashing ever $\frac{1}{30}$ second. You can see that the distance Jillian falls every $\frac{1}{30}$

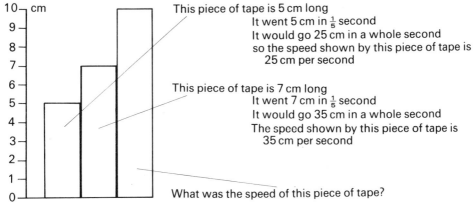

This piece of tape is 5 cm long
It went 5 cm in $\frac{1}{5}$ second
It would go 25 cm in a whole second
so the speed shown by this piece of tape is
25 cm per second

This piece of tape is 7 cm long
It went 7 cm in $\frac{1}{5}$ second
It would go 35 cm in a whole second
The speed shown by this piece of tape is
35 cm per second

What was the speed of this piece of tape?

Fig. 4.26   Working out the speed from a piece of tape

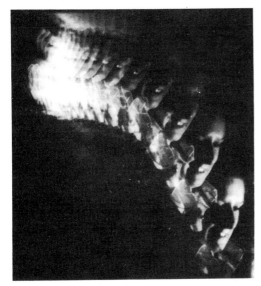

Fig. 4.27   A stroboscopic photograph of Jillian jumping from a stool

Fig. 4.28   A trolley on a runway

second is getting larger, as she gets nearer the floor.

As well as measuring speed, physicists also need to measure acceleration. To learn how to do this it would be best if you had a tape chart of something that accelerated evenly, or, in other words, was moving with *constant acceleration*. The easiest thing to use is some sort of trolley rolling down a slope as in Fig. 4.28.

Set up the apparatus shown in Fig. 4.28. Make the high end of the runway about 30 cm higher than the low end. Pass one end of a 2 metre length of tape through the timer, attach the tape to the trolley, switch on the timer and let the trolley roll down the slope without pushing the trolley. Make a tape chart in the same way as you did before.

4.12 Measuring acceleration

To *measure* acceleration, physicists calculate the *change* in speed every second (or occasionally, in another unit of time). For example, the cheetah in Fig. 4.14 might be running at 30 m/s on one occasion, and a second later it might be running at 35 m/s. It will have changed its speed by 5 m/s in that second, so the cheetah's acceleration is 5 m/s in one second.

As another example, a car might accelerate from 10 km/hr to 22 km/hr in 6 seconds. Its *change* in speed would be 22−10 = 12 km/hr. Its average change of speed every second is 12/6 = 2 km/hr, so its average acceleration is 2 km/hr every second. (There is that word 'average' again. Why is it there?)

You can measure the acceleration of your trolley from your tape chart. Fig. 4.29 shows you how. Measure the average speed shown by the first piece of tape in the same way as you did for your last tape chart. Write this speed on your chart. Then find the piece of tape which was made 1 second later (5 pieces later—why?) Find the speed shown by this piece of tape. Calculate the *change* in speed between the two pieces of tape. Since this change took place in 1 second, what you have calculated is the acceleration.

Sometimes a tape chart might span two or more complete seconds, like the one in Fig. 4.30. In this case you can find the change of speed over a longer time and then divide by the number of seconds to find the average change for every second.

Suppose your chart represents *less* than 1 second? Fig. 4.31 shows you what to do in this case.

From these examples you should be able to see that you can always *calculate* the acceleration of something from the equation:

$$\frac{\text{average}}{\text{acceleration}} = \frac{\text{change in speed}}{\text{time taken for speed to change}}.$$

4.13 What makes things accelerate?

An important question! In fact, it is the first important physics question we have had in this book for many pages. It is a little easier to think about what *stops* things that are moving than to think about what makes stationary things start to move. Look at the curved curtain rail illustrated in Fig. 4.32. Paul is about to release a marble at the top of one side.

Fig. 4.29   Measuring acceleration from a tape chart

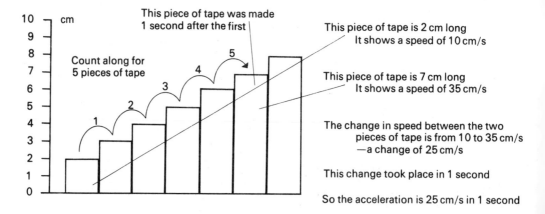

10 cm

This piece of tape was made 1 second after the first

This piece of tape is 2 cm long
It shows a speed of 10 cm/s

Count along for 5 pieces of tape

This piece of tape is 7 cm long
It shows a speed of 35 cm/s

The change in speed between the two pieces of tape is from 10 to 35 cm/s
—a change of 25 cm/s

This change took place in 1 second

So the acceleration is 25 cm/s in 1 second

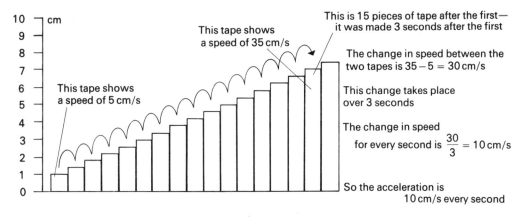

Fig. 4.30   Measuring acceleration over several seconds

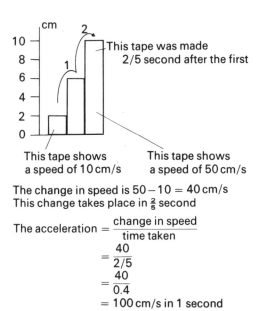

This tape shows
a speed of 10 cm/s

This tape shows
a speed of 50 cm/s

The change in speed is $50 - 10 = 40$ cm/s
This change takes place in $\frac{2}{5}$ second

The acceleration $= \dfrac{\text{change in speed}}{\text{time taken}}$

$= \dfrac{40}{2/5}$

$= \dfrac{40}{0.4}$

$= 100$ cm/s in 1 second

Fig. 4.31   Measuring acceleration from a chart
which spans less than one second

Gravity will accelerate it down the slope; the marble will decelerate as it goes up the other side. Fig. 4.33 shows where Jillian caught the marble where it stopped at the other side. Obviously gravity made the marble decelerate because it was pulling the marble back down the slope, but is gravity the only force to think about? Notice that the marble did not quite reach the same height from which it started—it did not quite get back all its gravitational potential energy. Some of it was permanently changed into another form of energy. Why?

If the curtain rail was arranged as in Fig. 4.34, the marble would accelerate down the hill as before, but then it would slow down on the level part even though gravity cannot be slowing it down this time. Why does it slow down? The

Fig. 4.32   Paul is about to release
the marble

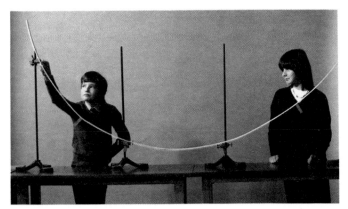

61

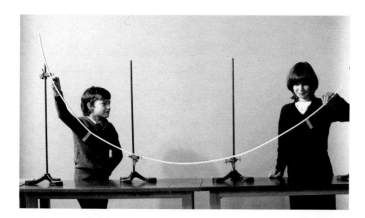

Fig. 4.33 Jillian has caught the marble at the greatest height to which it rose

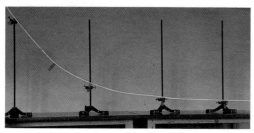

Fig. 4.34 How far will the marble go on this curtain rail?

Fig. 4.35 Why does Jillian eventually stop when she stops pedalling?

answer to both questions is the same as the reason why Jillian (Fig. 4.35) will eventually slow down and stop when she stops pedalling—**friction**.

Suppose there was no friction. Does that mean that the marble would keep going along the level part of the curtain rail for ever without slowing down? (Imagine a very long curtain rail!) Physicists think that the answer to this question is 'yes'—without any force pushing or pulling something it will either keep going for ever at constant speed, or it will not move at all if it is already still.

It is virtually impossible to have frictionless motion. The apparatus in Fig. 4.36 is able to provide the closest approximation to frictionless motion that you are likely to see. It is called an **air track**. Air is blown out through small holes (usually by means of a vacuum cleaner arranged to blow rather than suck) so that the specially shaped vehicle rides on a cushion of air. Once moving, the vehicle keeps going without any change of speed.

Fig. 4.36 An air track. The 'vehicle' rides on a cushion of air

It was Galileo (whose name you have already met—in what connection?) who first wrote about the ideas mentioned in this section. These ideas form the basis of the first of Newton's three laws of motion: 'If no unbalanced forces push or pull a body, then that body will stay still or keep moving with constant velocity. An unbalanced force will cause a body to accelerate.'

The word 'unbalanced' has been used twice. What does it mean? Why is it necessary to use the word here?

4.14 Force and acceleration

Now you know that to accelerate something you need a force to push or pull it, the next obvious question is, how much force? Obviously, this depends on how much acceleration you want. In what way does the acceleration depend on the force? If you double the force, do you double the acceleration, or quadruple the acceleration, or what?

The easiest apparatus to use to investigate this problem is the trolley and runway that you have already met. You can use a timer to measure the acceleration of the trolley, but how are you going to pull the trolley so that you can double the pull or treble the pull when you want to? In other words, you want to be able to have one unit of force, or two units of force, or three units of force.

Fig. 4.37   Pulling a trolley with one elastic

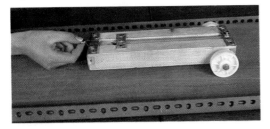

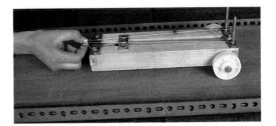

Fig. 4.38   Pulling a trolley with two elastics

One possible way is to use a piece of elastic attached to the back of the trolley as in Fig. 4.37. This can be pulled so that the front of the elastic is level with the front of the trolley as in the photograph. The elastic will then be providing a force to pull the trolley. If the elastic is always pulled the same amount then there is always the same force pulling the trolley. Two units of force can be provided by two elastics of the same length side by side as in Fig. 4.38, three units of force by three elastics, and so on.

Unfortunately, the pieces of elastic are not the only forces on your trolley. There is also friction trying to slow the trolley down. What can you do about this? You cannot get rid of the friction altogether, but you can *compensate* for it by having just a little bit of *extra* force forwards which just balances the friction force pulling backwards. You can get this extra force by arranging the runway on a *slight* slope, so that gravity pulling the trolley down the hill just balances the friction pulling backwards. The slope only needs to be a slight one. To test if you have the right slope, stand a trolley on the runway. It should not move off on its own, but if it is given a small push to start it going down the slope, it should keep going down at a constant speed. This test should be done with the tape through the timer and attached to the trolley. Why?

The trolley is now on a **friction-compensated slope**. Attach a piece of ticker-tape that passes through a timer. Switch on the timer and accelerate the   63 trolley using one elastic. You may first need to practise pulling the trolley so that the elastic stays stretched by the same amount all the time. Make a chart from your ticker tape and measure the acceleration in the way you have already learned.

Repeat this for two elastics, three elastics and even four elastics if you have time, although you might find it hard to keep pace with the trolley. Make a tape chart in each case and measure the acceleration.

Record your results in a table like the one shown below.

Force (no. of elastics)	Acceleration (cm/s every second)
0	
1	
2	
3	

To save time you might prefer to work in a big enough group so that one person accelerates the trolley with one elastic, and makes that tape chart. Another person deals with two elastics, and so on. Pool your results at the end.

When you have finished, it is a good idea to compare your results with other groups in your class working on the same experiments. Does each group have identical results? Most of the results from different groups will probably be similar, but there might be one or two *big* differences. These mean that somebody has made a mistake somewhere, such as not working out an acceleration correctly. Apart from these, why are the rest of the results not the same? Write down any reasons you can think of for the differences between the results of the different groups.

Do you think it is a good idea to average the results of all the groups? Would you include the 'very different' results in your average? Give reasons for your answers. If you think it *is* a good idea to average the results of all the groups, then do so.

Can you come to any conclusion from your results? Can you answer the question that was asked at the beginning of this section? Quite possibly not, because it is not always easy to see from a set of numbers exactly what is happening. Scientists often obtain a better picture of their results by drawing a *graph*.

Draw a graph of force (up the side) against acceleration (along the bottom). Fiona's graph is shown in Fig. 4.39 to help you if you are not quite sure what to do.

Notice that the graph should have a *title*, have each axis *labelled* with what is being plotted, together with the units (e.g. 'acceleration in cm/s every second') as well as having numbers along each axis.

Look again at Fig. 4.39. Why has Fiona drawn a straight line which misses most of the points? Shouldn't she have joined up all the points? What are you going to do about drawing a line on *your* graph?

What does your graph tell you about the way the acceleration depends on the force? The graph illustrated shows that if Fiona doubled the force from one to two elastics, then the acceleration doubled from 28 cm/s every second to 56 cm/s every second. Trebling the force from one to three elastics trebled the acceleration from 28 cm/s every second to 84 cm/s every second. Does your graph tell the same story?

If doubling the force doubles the acceleration, then we say that the acceleration is *directly proportional to* the force. A graph of two quantities that are directly proportional to each other will always be a straight line passing through the origin, as in Fiona's graph.

Newton concluded that force and acceleration are directly proportional to each other, and part of his second law of motion says just that.

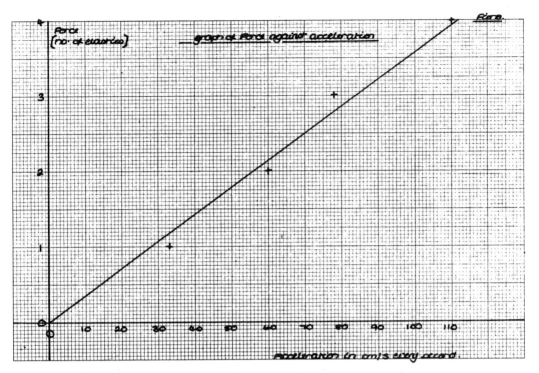

Fig. 4.39   Fiona's graph of force against acceleration

4.15   Mass and acceleration

How hard you push something is not the only thing that affects its acceleration. The mass of an object affects its acceleration. It is harder to accelerate a large, massive object, like an elephant, than a small, light one, like a mouse. Try to design an experiment, similar to the last one, to investigate this. If you succeed, you will have found the other half of Newton's second law of motion. His third law will have to wait for a while, though.

_____SUMMARY_____

Now that you have finished studying this chapter on motion, there are a number of things you should know and be able to do.

1 You should:
  a) be able to judge which is the best 'clock' for a particular job;
  b) be able to use a stopclock accurately to time a swinging pendulum;
  c) know that

$$\text{speed} = \frac{\text{distance travelled}}{\text{time taken}};$$

  d) know that

$$\text{acceleration} = \frac{\text{change of speed}}{\text{time taken}};$$

  e) know how to measure speed using a stopclock and ruler;
  f) know how to use a ticker-tape timer;
  g) be able to make a tape chart;
  h) be able to measure velocity and acceleration from a tape chart;
  i) be able to draw graphs;
  j) know what stroboscopic photography is;

k) know Newton's first law of motion (something will keep moving at constant velocity unless there is an unbalanced force on it);
l) know what 'direct proportionality' means;
m) know that a graph which is a straight line passing through the origin shows that the two quantities being plotted are directly proportional to each other.
n) know that the acceleration of something is proportional to the unbalanced force on it.
2 You should know what each of the following is, or what each does:
pendulum   stroboscope

mainspring   average
cine camera   friction
velocity   air track
acceleration   unbalanced force
deceleration   friction-
                      compensated
                      slope
3 These are some of the other words that have been used in this chapter. You should know what each word means:
primitive   calculate
civilization   permanent
regulate   illuminate
oscillate   retard
vibrate   constant
compare   compensate

FURTHER QUESTIONS

1 How could you tell if time suddenly started going backwards?
2 Describe how you would measure the speed of the hare in Fig. 4.12. Say what measurements you would make and how you would make them.
3 Calculate the missing figures in the following table. Remember to put in the correct units (metres, km/hr, or whatever is appropriate).

Distance covered	Time taken	Speed
10 m	5 s	(a)
6 km	2 hr	(b)
150 km	3 hr	(c)
(d)	2 s	6 m/s
(e)	4 hr	3 km/hr
25 cm	(f)	5 cm/s
50 m	(g)	10 m/s
2 m	$\frac{1}{2}$ s	(h)
5 km	$\frac{1}{4}$ hr	(i)
(j)	0.1 s	20 m/s

4 The diagrams in Fig. 4.40 show four different tape charts made by cutting up a tape every ten dots and sticking the tapes side by side. The vibrator made 50 dots every second.

a) Describe the kind of motion shown by each of these tape charts.
b) How much time does it take to make each piece of tape with ten dots on it?
c) Which tape showed the highest speed? What was that speed?
d) Which tape showed the slowest speed? What was that speed?
e) How far did the object pulling each tape go?
f) For how much time was each tape pulled through the timer?
g) What is the average speed of each object pulling the tapes?
h) For tape (A), the average speed you have found is the constant speed at which the object was moving all the time. Did tape (B) ever move at the average speed that you have calculated for this tape? If so, how many times?
5 Fig. 4.41 shows various tape charts.
a) Which tapes show acceleration?
b) Which tapes show deceleration?
c) Which tapes show no acceleration?
d) In chart (A) what is the average speed shown by the first piece of tape? (The timer taps 50 dots/s.)
e) What is the average speed shown

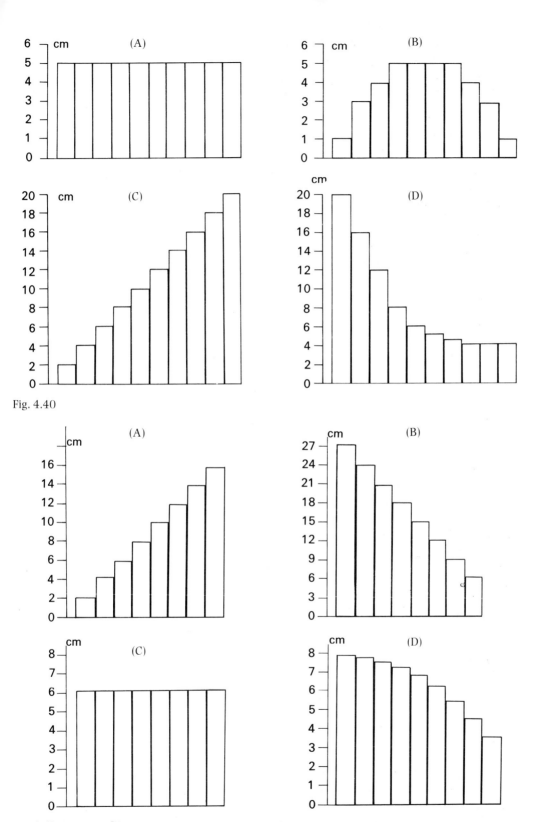

Fig. 4.40

Fig. 4.41

by the piece of tape made a second later (i.e. the 6th length of tape)?

f) What was the change of speed over this one second?

g) What, then, was the acceleration shown by chart (A)?

h) Work out the acceleration of any other tapes which show constant acceleration or deceleration.

6 The readings on the speedometers of three cars were taken every 5 seconds and recorded in the tables below.

a) By how much does the Mini increase its speed every 5 seconds? How much increase is this for every second? What is the Mini's acceleration?

b) What is the Escort's acceleration?

c) What is the Range Rover's acceleration?

Mini

Time (seconds)	0	5	10	15	20
Speed (km/hr)	10	13	16	19	22

Ford Escort

Time (seconds)	0	5	10	15	20
Speed (km/hr)	15	15	15	15	15

Range Rover

Time (seconds)	0	5	10	15	20
Speed (km/hr)	40	30	20	10	0

d) If the Mini continued with the same acceleration, how fast would it be moving after 30 seconds?

e) How fast do you think the Escort

will be moving after 30 seconds?

f) It is unlikely that the Range Rover will keep going with the same acceleration after 20 seconds. Why? How fast would it be going at 30 seconds if it did keep going with the same acceleration?

7 a) A locomotive pulling a train on a flat, horizontal track at 40 km/hr without accelerating needs to exert a force (it has to pull). Why is this? What is the force for if it is not to accelerate the train?

b) If the train is moving at a faster constant speed (say 70 km/hr) then the locomotive needs to exert a *larger* force than when moving at 40 km/hr. Why?

8 Why do scientists usually find it useful to draw a *graph* of a set of results?

9 The following table shows the number of bananas ordered by a zoo in order to feed its monkeys over a ten week period. The number of monkeys in the zoo varied quite a lot in this time! Draw a suitable graph to find out if the number of bananas ordered was proportional to the number of monkeys in the zoo.

Week	Number of monkeys	Number of bananas
1	4	60
2	4	60
3	6	90
4	7	100
5	4	60
6	2	30
7	2	30
8	5	75
9	7	100
10	8	110

10 When you sit on a chair, there is a force pulling you down (your weight). You have learnt that a force will cause something to accelerate. Why does the force pulling you down not make you accelerate?

5

MAINLY GASES
MAINLY GASES
MAINLY GASES

Fig. 5.1   Amethyst crystals

Fig. 5.2   Do all copper sulphate crystals look like this one?

5.1   Crystals

Look at Fig. 5.1. This photograph shows some amethyst **crystals** as they were dug from the ground. Suppose you were asked to describe these crystals to a friend over the telephone; your friend has never seen any crystals before. You cannot show your friend the photograph. What

Fig. 5.3   An alum crystal

would you say to your friend in order to describe completely these crystals?

Now look at some copper sulphate crystals and some potash alum crystals.   69

Look at as many different sizes as possible. A hand lens will be useful for looking at the small ones. Do all the copper sulphate crystals look the same? Do they look the same as the alum crystals? Figs 5.2 and 5.3 might help you.

Copy the following table and write down all the similarities and all the differences that you can see between copper sulphate and alum crystals.

Similarities between copper sulphate and potash alum crystals	Differences between copper sulphate and potash alum crystals

The beautiful shapes of snowflake crystals (Fig. 5.4) are made when water vapour in the air freezes.

Fig. 5.4   A snowflake

5.2   Watching hypo crystals grow

Crystals are often formed when a substance solidifies—changes from a liquid to a solid. You can easily watch crystals of hypo being made in this way. (You have probably heard of hypo; it is used in the developing of photographs.)

Put two or three spatula measures of hypo in a test tube. Warm them gently over a Bunsen flame until they have *just* melted. Put the test tube in a rack to let the molten hypo cool down. It might start to crystallize as it cools down, but you will probably have to wait until it is cool enough to touch and then drop in one crystal of hypo to start the rest of the hypo crystallizing. Watch carefully as the crystals form. You will find a hand lens useful.

5.3   Explaining the shape of crystals

How are you going to explain the regular shapes, the flat sides and the sharp corners you saw when you looked at crystals? The following simple experiment will help.

You need 30 polystyrene spheres, or marbles, or any other spheres that are all the same size. Arrange 16 of these spheres in a square on the bench as in Fig. 5.5. Use books or rulers at the edges to stop the spheres rolling around.

Put a second layer on top of this first layer. You will find that you need 9 spheres and that they fall naturally into place. Complete your pile of spheres with a third layer of 4 spheres, and one on top. What is the name of the shape you have made?

Fig. 5.5   A layer of 16 spheres

Fig. 5.6   Does the shape of this pile of spheres
look like any crystal you have seen?

scope, are called **atoms**. There is only one sort of atom in the diamond in Fig. 5.7—carbon—but in many substances atoms combine together in groups to form **molecules**. For example, carbon dioxide particles are molecules made of one atom of carbon combined with two atoms of oxygen.

Fig. 5.7   This diamond is made from only one
kind of atom—carbon

Compare this shape with the shape of an alum crystal. What do you notice? Is it possible that the alum crystal is made up of millions of tiny particles packed together in a regular way, like your pile of spheres? Physicists believe that this is so, and that this is one of the pieces of evidence that make scientists think that matter is made up of particles. It does not *prove* matter is made up of particles; it might be possible to think of another explanation for the shapes of crystals.

In the rest of this chapter you are going to look at some of the other evidence that makes scientists think that matter is made of minute particles. These minute particles, which cannot be seen, even with the most powerful **optical micro-**

Although it is not possible to see atoms with an optical microscope it is now possible to make an electron microscope which is powerful enough to see individual atoms. In Fig. 5.8(a) the black points are individual atoms of platinum whilst Fig. 5.8(b) shows molecules in a crystal. In both pictures the particles are arranged in a regular way just as scientists always thought they were.

5.4   Models

Physicists would call the pile of spheres which you made, a **model** of a crystal. You might think of a model as a *smaller* copy of something, like a model boat or aeroplane. Your model is a *larger* copy of   71

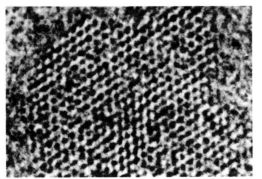

Fig. 5.8(a)   Atoms of platinum (magnification ×10 million)

Fig. 5.8(b)   Molecules in a crystal. Notice the regular arrangement (magnification ×2 million)

what we think a crystal looks like. Scientists often use enlarged models of things they cannot easily see to help to understand or explain them better. Of course, a model is not *exactly* like the original in all respects. A real aeroplane might be built mostly of aluminium, but a model might be made in plastic. Atoms are not really made from polystyrene!

Fig. 5.9   A model aeroplane

Fig. 5.10 shows a model of a salt crystal. Is it the same shape as the salt crystals that you put on your dinner? Notice that there are two different sizes of particle in the model. Can you suggest a reason for this?

5.5   Diffusion

Half fill a 250 ml beaker with water, stand the beaker on the bench and wait a few seconds for the water to stop moving. Put a straw in the water and drop a

Fig. 5.10   An enlarged model of a salt crystal. Why are there two different sizes of particle?

crystal of potassium permanganate down the straw to the bottom of the beaker (Fig. 5.11). Do not disturb the beaker for 15 to 20 minutes, but look at it frequently to see what happens. Write down what you notice.

How can you explain your observations. Try building the following simple model of the experiment. Into the bottom of a large beaker put a layer of coloured beads or marbles. These represent the particles of potassium permanganate. On top of these put several layers of white beads [Fig. 5.12(a)] to represent the water particles. Put the beaker on the bench. Do the beads mix together? Obviously not! But if you shake the beaker, so the beads can move about, the two kinds of beads

Fig. 5.11   The potassium permanganate has just been dropped down the straw. Will it look like this in an hour's time?

will mix together and will look like Fig. 5.12(b).

But did anyone shake your potassium permanganate solution? No—you took great care to make sure it was *not* disturbed. How then did the particles mix

Fig. 5.12   Mixing coloured spheres

(a)   (b)

together? We have to assume that the particles in a liquid are moving by themselves, and so can mix together by themselves. This is called **diffusion**.

Where do you think the particles get the energy from in order to move around?

5.6   Diffusion of bromine

A similar experiment to the last one, but using gases instead of liquids, can be done with bromine and air. Bromine is a brown liquid at room temperature, but it easily **vaporizes** to give a brown, choking gas which is denser than air. This experiment is best done in a fume cupboard, and your teacher may well want to demonstrate it.

Put a little vaseline round the tops of two gas jars so that when they are put together they form a gas-tight seal. Pour a little bromine into the bottom of one gas jar and put the other gas jar (which, of course, is full of air) upside-down on top of the first as in Fig. 5.13. Leave them

Fig. 5.13   There is bromine at the bottom of the gas jar, with air above. Will it look like this an hour later?

for at least an hour (a day if possible) without disturbing them, but look at what is happening every so often. Write down what happens to the bromine. Try to think of an *explanation* for what you see.

Do solids mix together by themselves? Would you expect the nut and bolt in Fig. 5.14 to diffuse into each other? Does this tell you anything about what the particles in a solid are doing?

Fig. 5.14   Will this nut and bolt diffuse together?

5.7   Brownian motion

The idea that the particles in liquids and gases are moving about by themselves is an important one. There is another experiment that supports this theory. Although the molecules in the air, for example, are too small to be seen, if there were also some bigger bits of matter that

Fig. 5.15   Could small particles of air knock bigger bits of matter about?

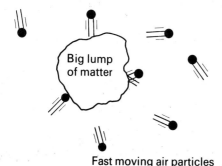

Big lump of matter

Fast moving air particles

can be seen in with the particles of air, these bigger bits might be knocked about by the moving particles of air. Fig. 5.15 illustrates the idea. You cannot make these bigger bits of matter too big, however, so you would have to use a microscope to see them.

Why would it be pointless trying to use very large lumps of matter as targets for the moving air molecules?

Smoke particles are used in the apparatus shown in Fig. 5.16. The smoke is put into a short piece of glass tubing (the **smoke cell**) which is illuminated from one side by a lamp. The glass rod acts as a lens to focus the light on to the smoke cell.

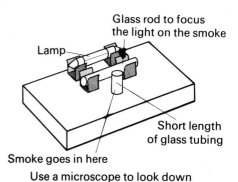

Glass rod to focus the light on the smoke

Lamp

Short length of glass tubing

Smoke goes in here

Use a microscope to look down the glass tube at the smoke

Fig. 5.16   Apparatus to look for bits of smoke being knocked about by air particles

The easiest way of making smoke is to light one end of a waxed straw. Hold the straw upright over the smoke cell, so the smoke falls down the straw into the cell. Place the assembly under a microscope (using a magnification of about 10) and light the lamp. Try to focus the microscope on the smoke, which will appear as very small, bright specks of light. It sometimes takes a while to find the smoke, and you may have to refill the cell before you are successful.

Describe exactly what your bits of smoke were doing. Draw a diagram if it helps your description. Can you explain why your bits of smoke were doing what you saw?

5.8 A model of Brownian motion

Fig. 5.18 shows a piece of apparatus that can be used to represent what is happening in Brownian motion. The clear plastic tube has in it a number of ball bearings and a larger piece of white polystyrene. The bottom of the tube is covered with a rubber membrane which is hit from underneath by a vibrating piston.

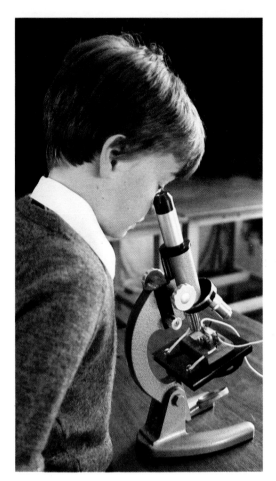

Fig. 5.17   Paul using the 'smoke cell' apparatus

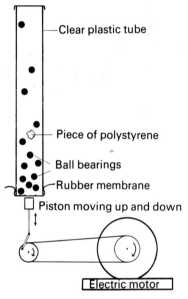

Fig. 5.18   A model for demonstrating Brownian motion

What you have just seen was first noticed in 1827 by a botanist called Robert Brown, except that he noticed the same effect with pollen grains suspended in water. He could not explain what he saw, and it was not until 1863 that a scientist called Wiener was able to explain that the 'jiggling' motion of the pollen grains was the result of their being knocked about by much smaller, invisible, but fast-moving water molecules. In just the same way, your bits of smoke were jiggling about because they were being bombarded by invisible, high-speed air particles. The jiggling of the lumps of smoke, or of the pollen grains, is called **Brownian motion**.

If possible, look at this apparatus while it is in action. (Fig. 5.19 was taken while the apparatus was in action, but obviously it is a still photograph (!) and is no substitute for looking at the real thing.) Answer the questions below.

1 What do you think the ball bearings represent?
2 What does the piece of polystyrene represent?
3 Look carefully at the piece of polystyrene. How would you describe the way it is moving? Why is it moving in this way?
4 Explain why this model represents what is happening in Brownian motion.

Fig. 5.19   Brownian motion model in action

5 Do you think this is a *good* model? Give a reason for your answer.

5.9   The states of matter

Look at Fig. 5.20. The ice, water and steam shown in this photograph look and feel very different to each other, yet all are made of the same *kind* of particles— water molecules (H_2O). The ice is **solid**, the water is **liquid** and the steam is a **gas**. Solids, liquids and gases are the three **states** of matter. Water is the most common substance that you are likely to meet in all three states.

Most other substances can be made into a solid, or a liquid, or a gas, although this is sometimes very difficult to do. Iron, for example, is something that is usually solid, but is melted to a liquid in an iron works (Fig. 5.21). It needs a *very* high temperature to make iron into a gas. To obtain this high temperature on Earth is very difficult.

Oxygen, on the other hand, is usually a gas. It can be liquified by cooling it to −183°C. Cooling liquid oxygen even

Fig. 5.20   Ice, water and steam—the three states of matter

further to −219°C will solidify it. These are very low temperatures.

You already know that in a solid the particles are packed very close together, like the model crystal in Fig. 5.10. This is why it is very difficult to squeeze something that is solid like ice or iron. But physicists believe that the particles are moving just a little, they are vibrating. This is something that the model of Fig. 5.10 cannot show. That is the trouble with models, they cannot show everything. A model with springs between the polystyrene balls, as in Fig. 5.22, would be better. This model has a fault too. The balls are too far apart—it is easy to squeeze this model. No model is perfect!

If a solid, like a lump of ice, is warmed up, the particles vibrate more and more, until they have enough energy to tear themselves away from their neighbours and move around. The solid has **melted**,

Fig. 5.21 Red-hot molten iron in a steel works

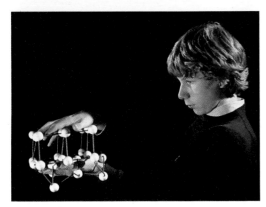

Fig. 5.22 A better model of a solid than that shown in Fig. 5.10—the spheres can move a little, but there is still something wrong with this model

The following paragraph is a summary of what scientists think about particles in the three states of matter. Copy out the paragraph, filling in the correct words where there is a choice.

'In a solid, the particles are *not moving/ vibrating a little/moving about all over the place*. In a liquid, the particles *are still close together/are a long way apart* and they are *not moving/moving* around. The particles in a gas are *close together/far apart* and are *moving around quite fast/not moving around at all*.'

5.10 The size of an olive oil molecule

How small are the atoms and molecules that make up all substances? This is not very easy to measure, but this experiment enables you to get a rough estimate of the size of a molecule of olive oil. The experiment makes use of the fact that, if a small drop of olive oil is put onto a clean water surface, the olive oil spreads out until it makes a layer one molecule thick. It is rather like pouring marbles onto a tray. They will tend to spread out so that there are no marbles piled on top of any others.

and become a liquid. The particles are still close together—a liquid is also difficult to squeeze, but the particles are free to move around.

As a liquid, like water, is warmed up, the molecules move around faster. Some move faster than others, and the fastest might escape from the liquid. We call this **evaporation**. Eventually all the molecules are moving fast enough to escape from each other and turn into a gas—the liquid **boils**.

Fill a tray to overflowing with water. It

77

is best if one end of the tray is over a sink. Wipe the surface of the water clean with a waxed rod as in Fig. 5.23. Sprinkle talcum powder, or lycopodium powder, over the surface of the water.

Fig. 5.23 Cleaning the surface of the water for the 'oil drop' experiment

You now need a drop of oil $\frac{1}{2}$ mm in diameter. Make one by dipping a U-shaped piece of wire into some olive oil so that there are a few drops on it, or perhaps just one at the bottom. Put this wire loop into a holder next to a ruler marked with $\frac{1}{2}$ mm divisions like the one in Fig. 5.24.

Fig. 5.24 Making the oil drop

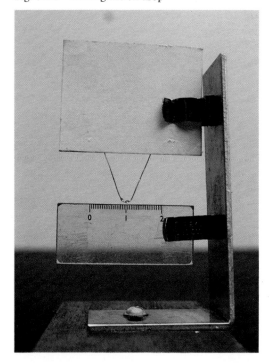

Try to make the drop of oil on the end of your loop $\frac{1}{2}$ mm in diameter by using a second loop to add oil to your first drop until it is just the right size. You will need to be patient, and look at what you are doing through a magnifying glass, as in Fig. 5.25.

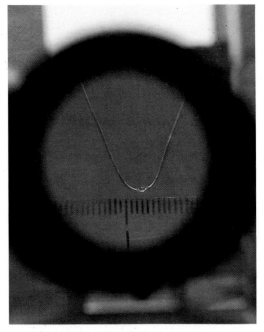

Fig. 5.25 A magnifying glass helps. Is this drop $\frac{1}{2}$ mm in diameter?

Dip the wire loop into the middle of the water in your tray so that all the oil comes off the wire and spreads out until it is one molecule thick. Measure the diameter of the patch of oil as soon as it is formed.

Since you are interested in a *rough estimate* for the size of the molecule it is helpful if you simplify the calculation and pretend the oil drop is a cube, with sides of length $\frac{1}{2}$ mm. You could also pretend that the patch of oil on the water is square, with sides of the same length as the diameter of the patch that you measured.

Fig. 5.26 shows you how to use your figures to work out the height of the patch of oil. Remember to use millimetres for measuring the diameter of the oil patch,

Drop of oil on wire loop

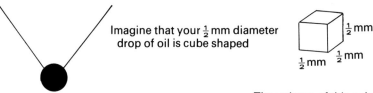

Imagine that your $\frac{1}{2}$ mm diameter drop of oil is cube shaped

$\frac{1}{2}$ mm

$\frac{1}{2}$ mm

$\frac{1}{2}$ mm

$\frac{1}{2}$ mm

The volume of this cube of oil is

$$\tfrac{1}{2} \times \tfrac{1}{2} \times \tfrac{1}{2} = \tfrac{1}{8} \text{ mm}^3$$

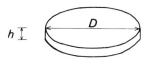

The drop of oil spread out to a roughly circular patch of oil on the water. The diameter of this patch was D.

h D

The height, h, of this oil patch is the length of an oil molecule

Imagine that this patch was square, with each side of the square being of length D

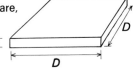

h D D

Measure D in millimetres

The volume of this patch of oil is $D \times D \times h$

You know that you started with $\frac{1}{8}$ mm³ of oil, so the volume of this patch must be $\frac{1}{8}$ mm³

So $D \times D \times h = \frac{1}{8}$ mm³

So $\qquad h = \dfrac{1}{8} \times \dfrac{1}{D \times D}$ mm

Since you measured the diameter D of your patch, you can put your number in place of D and calculate the length, h of an oil molecule

For example, suppose you measured the diameter of your patch of oil to be 200 mm

Then $h = \dfrac{1}{8} \times \dfrac{1}{200 \times 200}$

$\quad = \dfrac{1}{8} \times \dfrac{1}{40000}$

$\quad = \dfrac{1}{320000}$ mm (or 0.0000031 mm)

Fig. 5.26   Calculating the length of a molecule of olive oil

since you measured the size of the drop in millimetres.

From what chemists can tell us about the way in which the atoms in an olive oil molecule are arranged, we know that atoms are about ten times smaller than an olive oil molecule.

The number that you have calculated for the size of a molecule is very small. It is a little difficult to put any sort of meaning to this number. Perhaps it would help if you knew that there are about 1 million atoms across the diameter of the full stop at the end of this sentence. One million is a very large number, and might be equally difficult to imagine! One million tea leaves, if laid end to end, would stretch for about 1 km. That is the same as 50 cricket pitches laid end to end. Can you imagine that? One million grains of icing sugar would stretch about 10 m— about the length of an average sized laboratory. But you can fit 1 million atoms across this full stop.

5.11 How does temperature affect the pressure of a gas?

Most of the rest of this chapter looks more closely at what gases do. You should have in your mind a picture of gases as being made up of millions of particles moving in random directions at high speeds. (The average speed of the air molecules in the room in which you are sitting is about 500 m/s. It would take about 10 minutes to travel from London to Manchester at this speed.)

Start this section of work by finding an empty tin such as a coffee or syrup tin. Push the lid on firmly. Put the tin on a

Fig. 5.27 A cricket pitch

Fig. 5.28 Imagine 50 cricket pitches

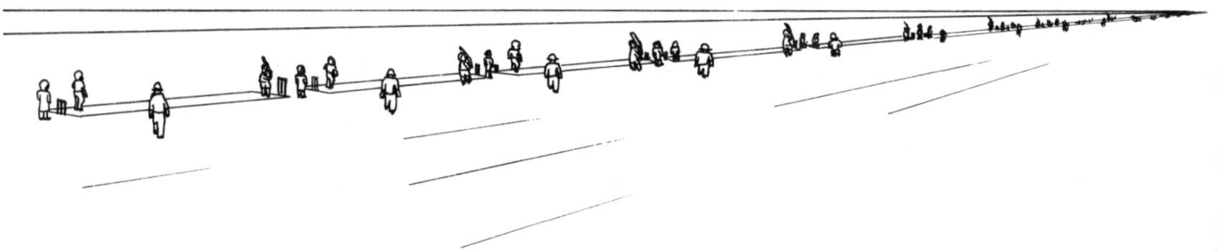

tripod over a Bunsen flame. Stand well back. (Your teacher may well want to demonstrate this experiment to you!) Write down what happens.

Why does this happen? I'm sure you will agree that the pressure in the tin has gone up, but why? If it comes to that, why should a gas exert a pressure at all?

The model that was used to illustrate Brownian motion can help again here. Fig. 5.29 shows the same model but without the lump of polystyrene. A piece of card (kept steady by a length of wire) has been put over the ball bearings. As the ball bearings bounce about they hit this card and so push against it, pushing with sufficient pressure to support it half way up the tube. If the ball bearings are given more energy, they will move faster,

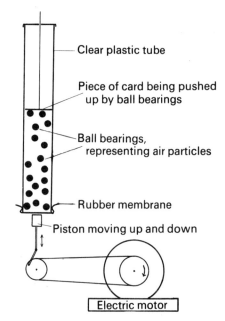

Clear plastic tube

Piece of card being pushed up by ball bearings

Ball bearings, representing air particles

Rubber membrane

Piston moving up and down

Electric motor

Fig. 5.29 A model to show why gas exerts a pressure

80

hit the card harder and so cause more pressure. How can you give the ball bearings in the model more energy? How can you give gas molecules more energy?

5.12 A relationship between temperature and pressure for a gas

Physicists are always on the lookout for simple patterns (or relationships) to help them make sense of the world around them. Is there a simple pattern to the way the pressure of a gas changes when the temperature is changed? To find out, you must carry out a more carefully controlled experiment than the one with the syrup tin, so that you can *measure* the pressure of the air at different temperatures.

Fig. 5.30 shows an apparatus suitable for this investigation. The air in the flask is slowly heated by the water in the can, which in turn is heated by the Bunsen

Fig. 5.30   How does the temperature of the air in the flask affect its pressure?

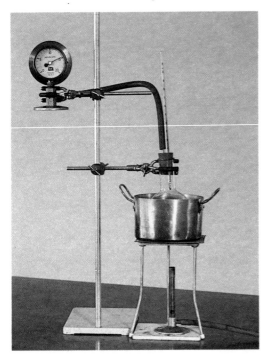

burner. The bung in the flask must be a snug fit, or some air will escape. There is a thermometer through the bung to measure the temperature of the air, while the pressure gauge measures the pressure of the air in the flask.

Assemble this apparatus. Put a mixture of ice and water into the can at the start so you can start at as low a temperature as possible. When the thermometer and pressure gauge have settled down, heat the water gently. Record the pressure of the air after every 10°C rise in temperature, and record your results in a table like the one below. It is a good idea to give the pressure gauge a gentle tap before you read it.

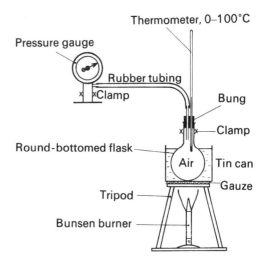

Fig. 5.31   How to draw a diagram of the apparatus in the previous photograph

Pressure (N/m²)	
Temperature (°C)	

To look for a pattern in your results, it is best to draw a graph, like the one in Fig. 5.32. Plot pressure up the side against temperature along the bottom. Does your graph show any pattern?

Does your graph show that the pressure is proportional to the temperature? In   81

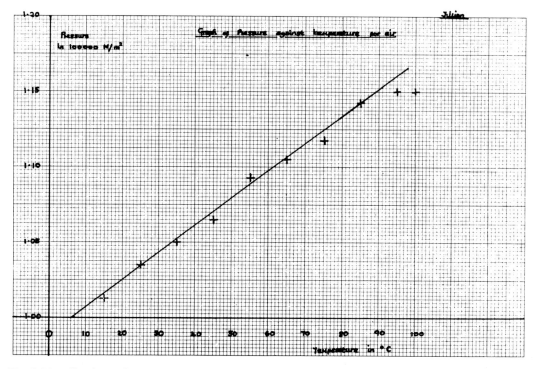

Fig. 5.32 Jillian's graph of pressure against temperature. Does this graph show that pressure is proportional to temperature?

other words, if the temperature doubles, say from 20°C to 40°C, does the pressure double? Does the graph in Fig. 5.32 show this? Explain your answers.

5.13 Absolute zero

Your graph shows that there is still a large pressure at a temperature of 0°C. The molecules of air are still bouncing around and knocking against the sides of the container. To what temperature would you have to cool the air so that the molecules stopped moving around and stopped causing any pressure? To find out, redraw your graph in the way shown in Fig. 5.33, continuing your line back to find the temperature at which there would be no pressure. What value do you obtain? Since at this temperature the molecules are not moving and so have no energy, this might be the lowest temperature that we can have.

Continuing a graph like this is called *extrapolating* the graph. You have to be careful about any conclusion which you reach. After all, any real gas would be a solid at this very low temperature, and the graph would not really carry on like this at all. However, when physicists carried out investigations similar to the one you have just done, they made a remarkable discovery. No matter what gas was used, and no matter how much was used, when extrapolated back the graph of pressure against temperature always gave the same answer for the temperature at which there would be no pressure and no movement of the molecules. Physicists think that this is the lowest obtainable temperature (and there is other evidence to support the idea). It is called **absolute zero**, and it is generally agreed that its value is −273°C.

How close was your value to −273°C? Why do you think your value did not exactly agree with this figure?

82

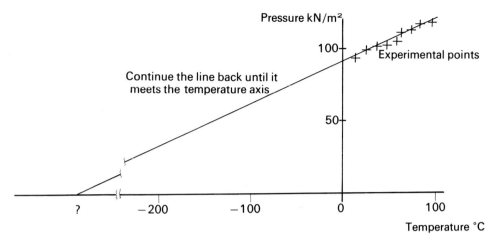

Fig. 5.33 Finding the temperature at which there would be no pressure

5.14   The kelvin temperature scale

Would it not be sensible if the lowest temperature, when molecules have no heat energy, was called '0' rather than '−273'? After all, we start measuring all other things like distance, or mass, on a scale that starts at '0'. So why not do the same for temperature?

Scientists *do* have such a temperature scale. It is called the **kelvin temperature scale** (or sometimes the **absolute temperature scale**). On this scale, 0 is at absolute zero and ice melts at 273 K. Fig. 5.34 shows the relationship between the kelvin temperature and centigrade temperature. (Notice that we write 273 K, for example, not 273°K.)

The kelvin temperature scale is not used for everyday temperature measurement; centigrade does very well for that. It is used by low temperature physicists, who might work with temperatures of only a few kelvin. It does have an important use for us in finding a pattern for the way in which the pressure of a gas depends on its temperature. Fig. 5.35 shows the graph of pressure against temperature in Fig. 5.33 redrawn with the temperature scale in kelvin. As before, the graph is still a straight line, but now it passes through the origin. What can you

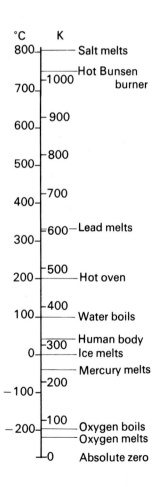

Fig. 5.34   Comparing the centigrade temperature scale with the kelvin scale

83

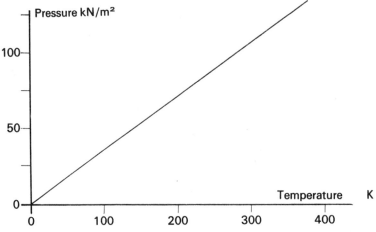

Fig. 5.35 A pressure/temperature graph with the temperature in kelvin

now say about the relationship between pressure and temperature? Answer by copying out the following sentence, filling in the blank space:

'The pressure of a given mass of gas is _____ to the temperature measured in kelvin, provided the volume stays the same.'

In the next section you will see why the phrase 'volume stays the same' has appeared.

5.15 The relation between the pressure and volume of a gas

One thing that scientists frequently do is to test their ideas with experiments. They think of what *ought* to happen on a particular occasion if their idea is right, and then carry out an experiment to see if it really does happen. You are about to do the same. In this section you are going to think of what ought to happen to some molecules of air in a box if the molecules really are moving about in the way you think. You are then going to do an experiment to see if what you expect really does happen.

Imagine that you have some molecules in a box as in Fig. 5.36. A pressure gauge connected to the box will measure the pressure due to these molecules. Now

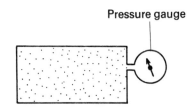

Fig. 5.36 A box of molecules

imagine that you put more molecules into the box, as in the next diagram.

1 What will happen to the number of times every second that the inside of the box is hit by moving molecules?
2 What, then, will happen to the pressure?
3 If you finish with twice as many molecules in the box as when you began, what do you think will have happened to the pressure?

Now you have thought of what *ought* to happen, you need an experiment to test your suggestion. But it is a little difficult to test your suggestion as it stands. You

Fig. 5.37 More molecules in the same box. What happens to the pressure?

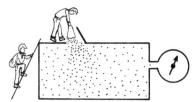

cannot *count* molecules as you put them into your box. However, you can obtain the same effect by pushing all the original molecules into a smaller volume, as in Fig. 5.38.

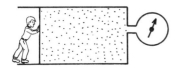

Fig. 5.38   The original number of molecules in a smaller box

How far do you think you would have to push in the side of the box in order to obtain the same effect as putting twice as many molecules into the big box?

You *can* test the answer to this question quite easily, using an item of apparatus like the one in Fig. 5.39. The 'box' is the closed glass tube with a scale (in cm³) behind it for measuring the volume of air in the tube. The 'movable side' of the box in Fig. 5.38 is a column of oil which can be pushed up using air pressure from a foot-pump. The pressure gauge records the pressure in the apparatus.

Scale in cubic centimetres

10	— Glass tube
20	
30	Pressure gauge
40	
50	
	To pump
60	— Oil

Fig. 5.39   Apparatus to investigate the effect of pressure on the volume of a gas

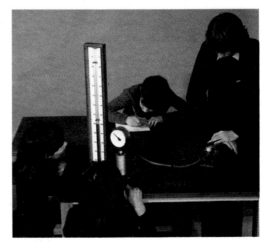

Fig. 5.40   The apparatus shown in Fig. 5.38 in use

Take a reading of the pressure, and of the volume of air. Gently pump some oil round so as to compress the air, and take another pair of readings. Repeat this for six more pairs of readings, recording your results in a table like the one below.

Pressure (N/m²)	
Volume (cm³)	

Draw a graph of pressure (up the side) against volume (along the bottom) using your results. Why is it sensible to draw a graph?

Does your graph show what you expected? Look at any pressure on your graph and write down the corresponding volume. Now look at double that pressure and write down the volume corresponding to this pressure. Has the volume halved as the pressure doubled? If the pressure trebles, does the volume reduce to a third of its original value?

If this happens then the pressure is *inversely proportional to* the volume. This means that if the pressure doubles then the volume halves.

This is a rule which applies to all gases. Scientists call a rule like this a **law**. (Some

85

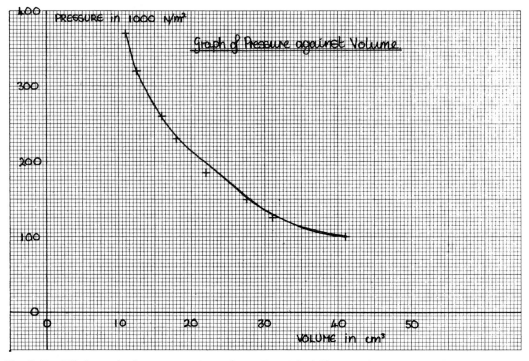

Fig. 5.41   Mike's graph of pressure against volume. Does it look like yours?

gases do not obey this law exactly.) What other scientific laws have you met?

Over 300 years ago Robert Boyle tried the same sort of experiment with apparatus which he designed and built himself. He used a piston of mercury to compress his sample of air. He hoped his experiments would help him improve the crude pumps that were being used to

Fig. 5.42   Robert Boyle

pump air down mines so that there was a continuous supply of fresh air for the miners to breathe. He discovered this law about pressure and volume in 1662, so we call the law 'Boyle's law'.

5.16   Inverse proportionality

The last section introduced you to the idea of inverse proportionality. This is an important idea in physics and it is worth exploring it in a little more detail. There are two further things you can do with your results of the last experiment which could increase your understanding of inverse proportionality.

Copy out your results again into a table like the one on the next page. In the third row write down the *reciprocal* of each of the volumes. The reciprocal of a number is 'one divided by that number'. For example, the reciprocal of 2 is $\frac{1}{2}$, or 0.5; the reciprocal of 8 is $\frac{1}{8}$, or 0.125. The word 'inverse' is sometimes used instead of reciprocal.

RESULTS FOR BOYLE'S LAW EXPERIMENT.   PAUL.

PRESSURE in 1000 N/m²	100	130	150	180	230	260	320	370
VOLUME in cm³	44	31	27.5	22	18	16	12.5	11
$\dfrac{1}{\text{VOLUME}}$		0.024	0.032	0.036	0.045			
PRESSURE × VOLUME	4400	4030						

Fig. 5.43   Some of Paul's results

Pressure (N/m²)	
Volume (cm³)	
1/V	
P × V	

Plot another graph, this time of pressure (up the side) against reciprocal of volume (along the bottom). Can you come to any conclusion from your new graph?

Now for some multiplication. Multiply each pressure by the corresponding volume, and put the result in the appropriate space in the fourth row. Do you notice anything about the numbers in the fourth row? Can you think of another way of writing Boyle's law?

5.17   Laws, models and theories

You have now met these words several times, and you should have some idea of what they mean.

A **law** is a rule. It tells you what things do. For example, Boyle's law tells you what happens to the volume of a gas if you change the pressure. Scientists discover laws by doing experiments and looking for patterns in the way things behave.

A **theory** is an idea, or a group of ideas, which tries to *explain* why things happen the way they do. For example, we can explain the way gases behave using the *idea* that gases are made up of particles that are moving about at high speeds in random directions. This idea is part of the *kinetic theory of gases*. Try to find out what the word 'kinetic' means and where it comes from.

A **model** is a copy of something that a scientist uses to help make an idea easier to understand or explain. Give details of one model you have met which has something to do with atoms and molecules, and details of any other scientific model you have met which has nothing to do with atoms and molecules.

87

Now that you have finished studying this chapter on gases, there are a number of things you should know or be able to do.

1 You should:
   a) be able to read a thermometer;
   b) be able to read a pressure gauge;
   c) be able to extrapolate a graph;
   d) have had more practice at drawing graphs;
   e) know that all matter is made up of minute particles;
   f) know that the particles in a solid vibrate, those in a liquid move around close to each other, while those in a gas fly around at high speed quite a long way from each other;
   g) know that models are sometimes used by scientists to help under-stand things too small to be seen;
   h) be able to explain diffusion;
   i) be able to explain Brownian motion;
   j) have a rough idea of the size of an atom;
   k) met the idea of absolute zero;
   l) understand the idea of inverse proportionality;
   m) know what the kelvin temperature scale is.

2 You should know what each of the following is, or what it does:

optical microscope   vapour
electron   evaporation
   microscope   model
crystal   law
atom   theory
molecule   states of matter

3 These are some of the other words that have been used in this chapter. You should know what each word means:

similarity   represent
difference   vaporize
                     extrapolate

FURTHER QUESTIONS

1 When bromine diffused into air in the experiment in Section 5.6, the diffu-sion was very slow. Yet physicists know that bromine molecules travel at a very high speed—about 200 m/s. Can you think of a reason why they mix so slowly with air even though they move so fast?

2 a) In the experiment to see Brownian motion of smoke particles, larger smoke particles would be easier to see. What two disadvantages would there be in using larger particles?
   b) If the air in the smoke cell in the Brownian motion experiment were hotter, would this make any difference to the motion of the smoke? Explain your answer.
   c) Explain whether a stronger light would make any difference to the motion.

3 If you release a little gas, bromine, for example, from a container, it will spread out to fill all the space available to it (it will mix with other gases to do so). There is no container round the Earth, yet the atmosphere does not seem to spread out into space. Can you suggest why this is so?

4 a) A kilogram of ice occupies about the same volume as a kilogram of water. From this, what can you deduce about the distance between the molecules in ice com-pared to the distance between them in water?
   b) A kilogram of steam occupies much more volume than a kilo-gram of water. What does this tell you about how the particles are spaced in steam compared with water?
   c) In fact, ice is a little less dense than

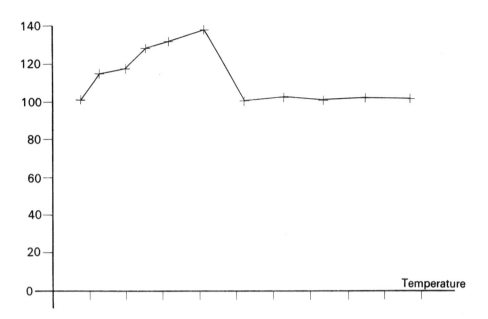

Fig. 5.44

water and so 1 kilogram of ice occupies a slightly larger volume than 1 kilogram of water. Suggest one piece of evidence for this statement.

5 A motorist measures the pressure in his car tyres before setting out on a long journey. The pressure is 270 kN/m^2. At the end of the journey the pressure is 300 kN/m^2. During the journey, what has happened to:
a) The number of molecules in the tyre?
b) The average speed of the molecules in the tyre?
c) The temperature of the gas in the tyre?

6 A pupil carried out an experiment like the one in Section 5.12 to find how the pressure of a gas changes with temperature. The pupil plotted the results on the graph shown in Fig. 5.44.
a) There are a number of things missing from this graph. What are they?
b) Suggest a reason for the rather odd shape of the graph.

7 This question refers to the apparatus in Fig. 5.30 used to investigate the relation between the pressure and temperature of a gas.
a) Why is it best if the tube between the flask and the pressure gauge is a narrow one?
b) Do you think it makes any difference to the experiment if a different sized flask is used?
c) Do you think it would make any difference to the experiment if the inside of the flask was wet?

8 A gas cylinder full of oxygen has a pressure of 500 kN/m^2 at a temperature of 0°C.
a) What is 0°C in kelvin?
b) Suppose the temperature was increased to 546 K. What would be the pressure in the gas cylinder?
c) What is 546 K in °C?
d) What would be the pressure of the oxygen at 100°C?
e) What would be the pressure of the oxygen at −50°C?

9 An oxygen cylinder in a hospital has a volume of 20 litres, and contains oxygen at a pressure of 1500 kN/m^2.

89

Atmospheric pressure is $100 \, kN/m^2$.

a) If the oxygen in the cylinder were allowed to expand until it was at atmospheric pressure, what volume of oxygen would there be?

b) In practice, how much of this oxygen would be available for use by patients?

10 Warning! This question uses big numbers! An oil tanker spills a cubic metre of oil. Work out how big the oil slick will be by answering the following questions.

a) How many millimetres are there in a metre?

b) How many cubic millimetres can you fit into a cubic metre? (Fig. 5.45).

c) The oil drop you used in Section 5.10 had, very roughly, a volume of 1/10th cubic millimetre. How many of your oil drops could you fit into a cubic metre?

d) If the oil from the tanker formed a slick of oil in the same way as your

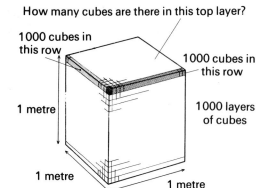

How many cubes are there in this top layer?

1000 cubes in this row

1000 cubes in this row

1 metre

1000 layers of cubes

1 metre

1 metre

Fig. 5.45

olive oil formed a patch of oil, how much bigger would the area of the oil tanker's slick be than your patch of oil?

e) Knowing the diameter of your oil patch, calculate a rough value for the diameter of the oil slick.

f) In actual practice, the oil slick would be much smaller than you have just calculated. Suggest a reason why.

6

OPTICAL INSTRUMENTS
OPTICAL INSTRUMENTS

OPTICAL INSTRUMENTS

Fig. 6.1　Rays of sunlight passing through smoke

6.1　Introduction

Look at the rays of sunlight passing through the smoke from the bonfire in the photograph. You must have seen this sort of thing for yourself before.

This chapter is about rays of light. Your eye would be a little useless without rays of light. But what does your eye *do* to rays of light so that you can see things? What do telescopes, magnifying glasses and spectacles, for example, do to rays of light so they can help your eye see things? What does a camera do to light rays so that it can take a photograph? Questions like this belong to the part of physics called **optics**, and in this chapter you are going to find some of the answers.

Look again at the rays of light in the photograph. Notice that they travel in straight lines, a fact we will use to explain how various optical instruments **work**.

What do you think 'optical instruments' are?

6.2　The pinhole camera

The kind of camera that Jillian is using in Fig. 6.2 is a very simple one, but you can find out several important things about rays of light by using it. It is easy to make.

91

Fig. 6.2   Jillian using a pinhole camera

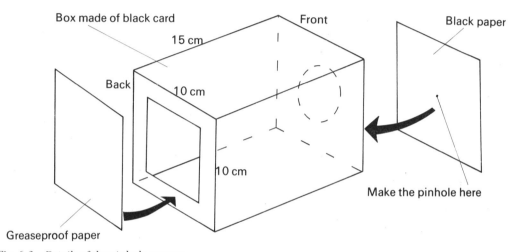

Box made of black card

15 cm

Back

10 cm

10 cm

Front

Black paper

Make the pinhole here

Greaseproof paper

Fig. 6.3   Details of the pinhole camera

Fig. 6.3 shows the details. It is a small cardboard box at the back of which there is a square hole. Cover this with grease-proof paper; this is the screen on which the camera makes a picture.

At the front is a round hole. Stick a piece of black paper over this hole. Use a pin to make a small hole in the middle of the paper. Stand about a metre away from a lamp (a special carbon filament lamp is best) and point the hole in the front of the camera towards the lamp. Look at the screen like Jillian is doing in the photograph. What do you see on the screen? Look carefully and draw a diagram of what you see.

The picture you see on the screen is called an **image** of the lamp.

Move towards the lamp. What happens

to the *size* of your image? Does anything else happen to your image?

Walk away from your lamp. What happens to the image this time?

Where do you have to put the camera so that the image is the same size as the lamp?

Now make a second pinhole in the black paper, beside the first. What do you see on the screen this time?

What do you see on the screen with half a dozen pinholes in the black paper?

Make a large hole with a pencil through the black paper at the front of your camera and describe what you see on the screen now.

How are you going to *explain* what you have seen? Start your explanation by copying Fig. 6.4. The top of the filament

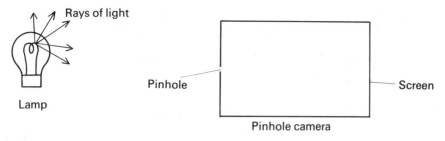

Fig. 6.4   How do you *explain* how the pinhole camera works?

in the lamp is sending out rays of light in all directions. Some of these rays have been drawn on the diagram. Only one of these rays can go through the very narrow pinhole at the front of the camera. Which one? Draw this ray on your diagram. Draw it going through the pinhole and going straight on until it hits the back of the camera. Remember that rays of light go in straight lines, so use a *ruler*.

Where does this ray of light hit the screen to make its bit of the image? Near the bottom or near the top?

The bottom of the filament is also giving out rays in all directions. One of these will go through the pinhole. Draw this ray, continuing it through the pinhole to the screen. Where does this ray hit the screen?

Complete the following paragraph.

'Rays of light from the top of the lamp go straight through the pinhole and finish at the _____ of the screen. Rays from the bottom of the lamp finish near the _____ of the screen. The image is *the right way up/upside-down.*'

Now draw another diagram, like Fig. 6.4, to show why it is that if the lamp is a long way from the camera, the image is comparatively small.

Why does a large hole make the image blurred? Look at Fig. 6.5. With this large hole many rays can get through into the camera, and each ray finishes in a different place on the screen. Rays of light starting at *one* point on the lamp form many *different* image points on the screen. It is like having many overlapping pinholes making many overlapping images.

6.3   The lens camera

If you were asked to take a photograph with your pinhole camera, you would think this was silly. But it is perfectly possible. Fig. 6.6 shows a photograph taken with a pinhole camera like the one in Fig. 6.2. Care had to be taken to make sure that no light could get in through the joins in the box, but it was not at all difficult to take this picture. A snag is that it took about 2 seconds to expose the film, if anything had moved in this time, it would have been blurred. The reason is that very little light gets through the

Fig. 6.5   Why does a large hole give a blurred image?

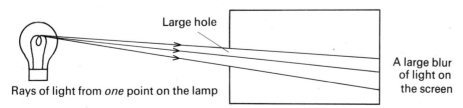

93

Fig. 6.6 Photograph taken using a pinhole camera

Fig. 6.7 Mike using a lens with a pinhole camera

pinhole, so the picture is very faint. We cannot get over this problem by making the pinhole bigger and so letting in more light. Why not?

All cameras used for taking photographs have a glass lens at the front. It is time to find out why. Use your pinhole camera again and stick a fresh sheet of black paper over the front. Make one pinhole in the paper. Point the camera at a lamp and hold a **convex** (or **converging**) **lens** in front of the pinhole as Mike is doing in Fig. 6.7. A convex lens is one that is thicker in the middle than at the edges. Does the lens make any difference to the image?

Make several pinholes in the black paper like you did before. Hold the lens in front of the holes and move it towards and away from the holes. Does this make any difference to the images?

Finally, use a lens with a large pencil hole in the paper. Write down what you see on the screen. Is the image the right way up?

Would this be a *better* camera for taking photographs? Why?

How can you *explain* what you have seen—what does the lens *do* to the rays of light? To answer this question, it would help if you could actually *see* the rays of light. One way to do this would be to pass the rays of light through a dusty or smoky atmosphere using apparatus like that in Fig. 6.8. Light from a lamp goes through a plate with holes in it to divide the light into rays, which then pass into a box full of smoke. Fig. 6.9 shows a view of the smoke box with the light rays passing into it.

Fig. 6.10 shows what happens if we put a lens in the box. It brings all the rays of

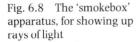

Fig. 6.8 The 'smokebox' apparatus, for showing up rays of light

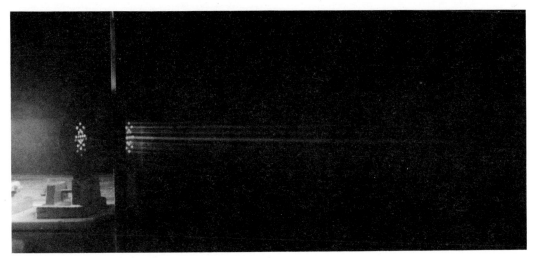

Fig. 6.9   Rays of light in a smokebox

light back together again. There is one point where they all cross. All the rays that left one point together (at the lamp) come together again to make one sharp image of that point. Fig. 6.11 shows the usual sort of **ray diagram** that a physicist might draw to show what is happening in the smoke box in Fig. 6.10.

6.4   The light rays kit

Although the smoke box can show the path of the rays of light quite well, I am sure you will agree that it is not the most *convenient* apparatus to use. Another way of showing up the path of rays of light is to use the apparatus shown in Fig. 6.12.

Fig. 6.10   Rays of light passing through a lens in a smokebox

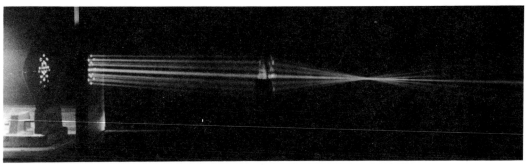

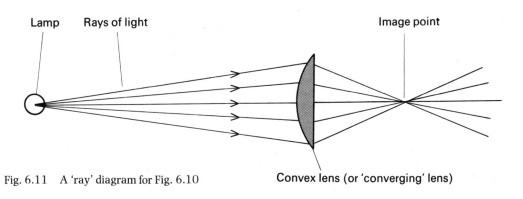

Lamp   Rays of light   Image point

Fig. 6.11   A 'ray' diagram for Fig. 6.10   Convex lens (or 'converging' lens)   95

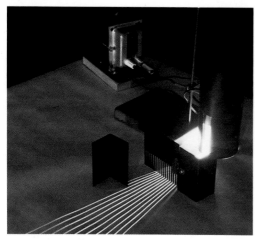
Fig. 6.12   The light rays kit

Light from the lamp passes through a lot of slits to divide it into rays. The path of the rays can be seen on the white paper on the bench. The apparatus uses special cylindrical lenses such as those shown in Fig. 6.13. These bend the rays in such a way that they stay on the paper.

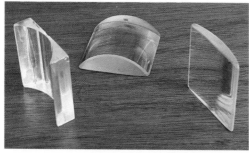
Fig. 6.13   Cylindrical lenses, for use with the light rays kit

This apparatus is a *simplification* of the real thing. The smoke box showed what happened in three dimensions, while this apparatus just shows two dimensions.

Set up the apparatus shown in Fig. 6.12. Adjust the height of the lamp, and the distance of the slits from the lamp to give the best rays, ones that go a long way across the paper. Put a convex lens in the rays of light and look at what happens. Draw a diagram to show what happens to the rays.

Try convex lenses of different thicknesses. What is the effect of different lenses on the rays? If possible, try a **concave lens** (one which is thinner in the middle than at the edges).

If the rays of light come together and meet after passing through the lens, the point at which they meet is called the **image point**. Since all the rays *come* from one point (the filament of the lamp) they should come together at one point to form a sharp image. But look at Fig. 6.14. This shows an image point formed by one of the lenses, and it does not seem to be very good. The rays of light are not all crossing in the same place in this case. Did the same thing happen with your lenses? Did it happen more for one lens than another?

There is another thing wrong with the image in Fig. 6.14, particularly with the rays of light which pass near the outside of the lens. Can you see what it is? Did the same thing happen with your lenses?

Fig. 6.14   An image point made by rays of light passing through a cylindrical lens.

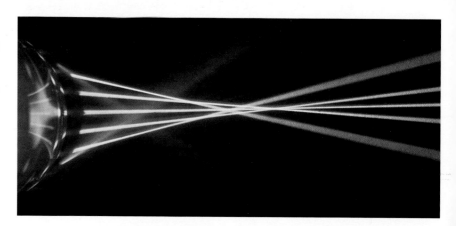

6.5 Camera lenses

If the rays of light passing through a lens do not all cross at one point, even though they have come from one point, then the image is going to be *blurred*. There is nothing wrong with the lens. This is just what lenses do to rays of light. It is a problem for the designer of a camera lens. People prefer sharp photographs to blurred ones.

There are two ways round this problem. Look again at Fig. 6.14 and notice that it is the rays that have come through the lens near the edges that are the worst problem. The easiest thing to do is not to use these rays at all, but just use the rays near the centre of the lens. This is called **stopping down** the lens. This is done in cheap cameras; a hole is put in front of the lens so that only the middle of it is used.

Try stopping down your lens using your light rays apparatus to see if the image improves. The snag is there is now less light going through the lens than if the whole lens were used. This is why cheap cameras can only take photographs in bright light.

The other solution to the problem is to use many lenses together, so that the defects in all the lenses cancel out. It is

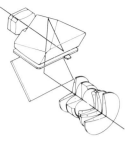

Fig. 6.15 The combination of lenses used in the camera in the next photograph

difficult to design a set of lenses like that, but it is how high-quality camera lenses are made. This is one reason why they are so expensive. Fig. 6.15 shows a diagram of all the lenses that go to make up the high-quality camera lens shown in the next photograph.

6.6 Focusing a camera

Set up your light rays kit as before and then move the lamp (the **'object'**) a little nearer the lens. The position of the image moves as well. Which way? Nearer to or further from the lens?

If a camera is to take a sharp photograph, the lens must be able to move so that it is the right distance from the film, depending on how far away the object is. This is called **focusing** the camera. In

Fig. 6.16   A high quality camera

(a)
(b)

Fig. 6.17 Old and new cameras. Notice the different ways of focusing them

older cameras, the lens was attached to bellows like the one in Fig. 6.17(a) so that it could be moved to the right distance from the film. With modern cameras a ring is turned on the lens casing to move the lens, as in Fig. 6.17(b).

In a simple camera the lens cannot be moved, and all objects beyond about 2 m are adequately in focus. You will see why shortly.

6.7 Getting the right exposure

Many cameras can be used to take successful photographs whether it is bright or dull. It has to be possible to adjust the camera so that the right amount of light falls on the film. All cameras have a **shutter** which opens to expose the film to light; one possible adjustment is to alter the time for which this shutter is open. Some cameras have a wide range of adjustments—from 1/1000 second to over 1 second, for example.

You can see the shutter time adjusting dial next to the main body of the camera in Fig. 6.16. (The shutter *time* is usually called the shutter *speed*. This is not the correct word to use, but all photographers use it.)

The other possible adjustment is the size of the hole, or **aperture**, through which the light passes into the camera. Fig. 6.18 shows the same lens with a wide aperture [Fig. 6.18(a)] which will let

Fig. 6.18 A camera lens showing a wide and a narrow aperture

(a)

(b)

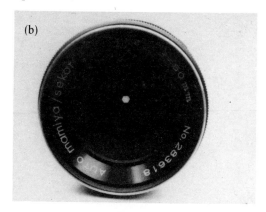

Fig. 6.19   This picture was taken through a lens with a small aperture

Fig. 6.20   This picture was taken through a lens with a wide aperture

There is another important effect of changing the aperture. Look at Figs. 6.19 and 6.20. Both photos were taken from the same place, but in Fig. 6.19, which was taken with a small aperture, the background is in focus as well as the foreground, while in Fig. 6.20, taken through a large aperture, the background is out of focus.

Do you think both pictures were taken with the same shutter time? If not, which was taken with the faster time, and why?

The range of distances that is in focus is called the **depth of focus** of the lens. An advantage of a simple camera is that, since, as you have seen, the lens has a narrow aperture, it has a large depth of focus. A simple camera is usually arranged so that any distance between 2 m and a very large distance ('infinity') is adequately in focus. For this reason, such a camera does not usually have to be focused.

Look at some of the other photographs in this book. Try to decide whether each was taken through a wide or narrow aperture. Can you guess which ones were probably taken using a fast shutter time?

through a lot of light, and with a narrow aperture [Fig. 6.18(b)] which will only let through a little light. Apertures are usually measured with an **f number**, e.g. f4, f5.6, f8, f11, etc. The larger the number, the smaller the aperture.

99

6.8 Summary of cameras

Complete the following paragraph as a summary of what you have learned about cameras:

'In a simple camera there is a *large/small* depth of field so *all/no* objects beyond about 2 m are reasonably in focus. This is because simple cameras have a *small/large* aperture. More complicated cameras have an aperture that can be changed; when the aperture is large the depth of focus is *small/large*. The lens in such cameras can be moved so the picture can be accurately focused. The lens is nearest the film when focused on *nearby/faraway* objects.'

6.9 Your eyes

Fig. 6.21

Your eyes are optical instruments that are in many ways similar to a camera. Fig. 6.22 shows a cross-section diagram of an eye, viewed from above. If possible, you

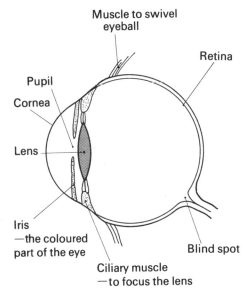

Fig. 6.22 The right eye, looking from above

Muscle to swivel eyeball

Retina

Pupil

Cornea

Lens

Iris
—the coloured part of the eye

Blind spot

Ciliary muscle
—to focus the lens

should dissect, or see dissected, a bull's eye, and look at the parts shown in Fig. 6.22.

Light goes into your eye through the clear **cornea**, passes through the lens and is focused to make a sharp image on the **retina** at the back of the eye. In the retina are nerve endings that are sensitive to light; some of them are also sensitive to colour. These nerve endings send messages to the brain via the **optic nerve**. Most of the bending of the light takes place at the cornea; the **lens** contributes a little to the bending, as shown in Fig. 6.23.

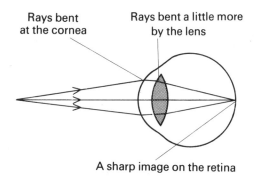

Rays bent at the cornea

Rays bent a little more by the lens

A sharp image on the retina

Fig. 6.23 The path of rays of light through the eye

The lens is surrounded by the **ciliary muscles,** which can squeeze the jelly-like lens to a fat shape, or relax to allow the lens to become thin. Why do you think the shape of the lens can be changed?

The inside of the eye is filled with a jelly-like liquid. Can you think why?

The inside of your eye is black. Can you think of a good reason for this?

The **iris**, which gives an eye its colour, has a hole in it called the pupil. This pupil can be made large or small. Why do you think the size of the pupil can be changed?

There are no nerve endings where the optic nerve leaves the eye. Your eye cannot see any image formed there. This is called the **blind spot**. To show you have a blind spot, close your left eye, hold this book at arm's length and look at the archer in Fig. 6.24. Concentrate on the

100

Fig. 6.24

archer, but you can also see his target out of the corner of your eye. Bring the book slowly towards you. At a certain distance the target disappears. Why?

Why does this not work if you do the same with your left eye? Why does your blind spot not usually bother you?

Why do you have two eyes? To answer this, take a pencil in each hand and hold them at arm's length as in Fig. 6.25. Close one eye, and try to bring the two pencil points together so that they touch. Then do it with both eyes open. Which is easier? Why?

Fig. 6.25

The lens in your eye does just the same thing to light as it does in your camera. This means that the image it makes on the retina is upside-down. Your brain has learned to interpret this correctly. After all, it has never known anything else!

6.10 The range of accommodation of your eyes

How close can you hold something to your eyes and still see it distinctly (without straining your eyes)? Try each eye separately. This closest point is called the **near point** of your eye.

Where is your **far point**—the furthest place at which you can see something distinctly? For many people, it is a long way off, or 'at infinity'.

The near point for many adults is about 25 centimetres, while their far point is infinity. The **range of accommodation** of their eyes is 25 cm to infinity. Younger eyes usually have a larger range of accommodation. A teenager's near point is usually closer than 25 cm. What is the range of accommodation of your eyes?

6.11 Defects of vision

For some people, the near point is considerably further away than 25 cm. They can see distant objects clearly but they are unable to focus on nearby objects; their view of a nearby book is rather like Fig. 6.26. To understand what is wrong, and what can be done about it, a model representing the eye is useful.

Fig. 6.26 A long-sighted reader's view of a book

Fig. 6.27 A model eye, made of a flask filled with fluorescein

Figs 6.30 and 6.31.) This is what is the matter with a **long-sighted** eye. The lens is not strong enough to focus rays from near objects to a sharp image on the retina.

This lens needs a little help by putting an extra convex lens in front of the eye, as has been done in Fig. 6.32. There is now a sharp image on the retina.

Thus a long-sighted eye needs a convex lens to help the eye lens focus on nearby objects. It could be a spectacle lens, or a contact lens which is placed on the cornea and is held there by the fluid round the eye.

For what reasons might a person wear contact lenses?

Short-sighted people have the opposite problem. Their eye lens can focus light from nearby objects to a sharp image (Fig. 6.34) but it is *too strong* for light from far objects (Fig. 6.35). Their view of a distant scene is like Fig. 6.36. What sort of spectacle lens do you think such a person needs? Draw a ray diagram, similar to Fig. 6.33, to show how your choice of lens will help a short-sighted person.

Fig. 6.27 shows a large flask filled with fluorescein solution. This glows green when light passes through it. The flask represents the eye. There is a lens stuck to the flask to represent the lens of the eye. Fig. 6.28 shows this lens focusing the light from a distant lamp to a sharp image at the back of the 'eye'. Fig. 6.29 shows a ray diagram of the same thing.

If this model eye 'looks at' a lamp that is nearer, the rays of light do not meet at the back. The lens is not strong enough to focus them on the back of the eye. (See

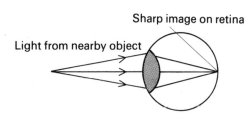

Fig. 6.34 A short-sighted eye looking at a nearby object

Fig. 6.28 and Fig. 6.29 Light being focused to a sharp image by a fluorescein 'eye'

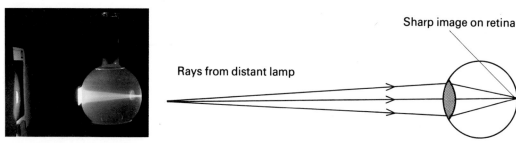

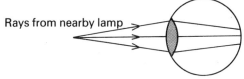

Lens cannot bend rays enough
to form sharp image on retina

Rays from nearby lamp

Fig. 6.30 and Fig. 6.31   A long-sighted fluorescein 'eye' looking at a nearby object

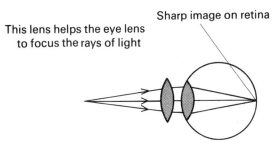

This lens helps the eye lens
to focus the rays of light

Sharp image on retina

Fig. 6.32 and Fig. 6.33   The long-sighted 'eye' with a correcting lens

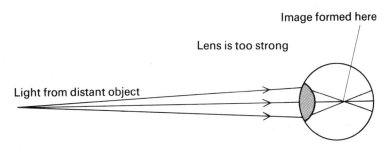

Image formed here

Lens is too strong

Light from distant object

Fig. 6.35   A short-sighted
eye looking at a distant
object

Fig. 6.36(a)   A short-sighted person's view of a
distant scene

Fig. 6.36(b)   A normal-sighted person's view of
the scene in Fig. 6.36(a)

6.12   More about lenses

Will a lens only make an image on the screen of a camera, as you did in Section 6.3? Of course not! Hold a lens towards a lamp (Fig. 6.37), and try to catch the image on a piece of paper, or on the wall. As with your camera, the image is probably smaller than the lamp. How could you make an image that is *larger* than the lamp? Where must you put the lens? A slide projector makes an enlarged image. Where is the lens on a slide projector in relation to the slide?

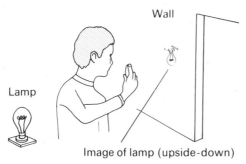

Fig. 6.37   A camera is not necessary for a lens to make an image

You can understand better how to make images of different sizes using the light rays kit. You will need to alter the apparatus a little. When you used this apparatus before, all the rays of light came from *one point*, and formed an image at *one point*—a **point image**. A point does not have a 'size'. Real objects and images do have a size—there is some distance between the top and the bottom of an image.

Fig. 6.38 shows how you can arrange the light rays kit to represent a real object. There are two lamps. One sends out rays from the top of the object. The other sends out rays from the bottom of the object. These rays have been made different colours in the photograph so you can see which is which. You can see there is a top and bottom to the image. Imagine that the rest of the image is between these two limits.

Set up this apparatus for yourself. Try to find out where to put the lens so that the image is the *same size* as the object. Measure and write down the distance from the lens to the object and from the lens to the image. What do you notice about your measurements?

Now move the lens so that the image is half the size of the object and measure the same distances. Repeat this for various other image sizes and record your results in a table like the one below.

Size of image compared to size of object	Distance from lens to object	Distance from lens to image
same size $\frac{1}{2}$ as big $\frac{1}{3}$ as big $\frac{1}{4}$ as big 2 times as big		

Fig. 6.38   Using the light rays kit to represent rays coming from the top and bottom of an object

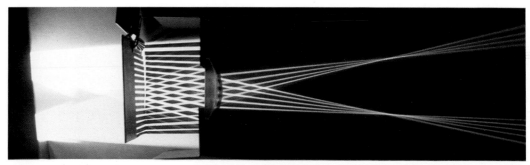

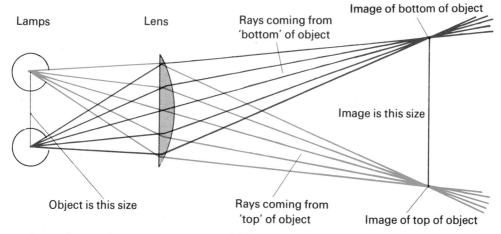

Fig. 6.39 Ray diagram for the apparatus in Fig. 6.38

Look at your results. Can you see any rule about how to calculate how much bigger the image is than the object? Physicists use the word **magnification** to mean 'how much bigger the image is than the object'. You could label the first column of your table 'magnification'.

Try to design and carry out an experiment to check whether the rule you have discovered also works with spherical lenses such as the one you used with your lens camera.

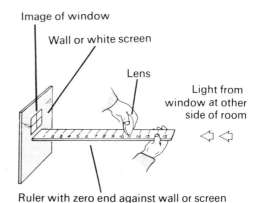

Fig. 6.40 Finding the focal length of a lens

6.13 Focal length and power of lenses

You already know that fatter convex lenses are more powerful than thinner lenses. You need a simple way of *measuring* the strength of lenses. This is done by focusing your lens on an object which is a long way off (the window on the far side of a large room is far enough away) and measuring the distance between the lens and the image as in Fig. 6.40. This distance is called the **focal length** of the lens.

Use this method to find the focal length of the lens you used for your camera.

Fig. 6.41 is a light rays kit model to show what is happening to the rays of light. Since the window is a long way off,

the rays coming from one point on the window which actually hit the lens are virtually *parallel*. Fig. 6.42 shows why this is so. The rays converge to form a point image at a point called the **focal point**. The distance from the focal point to the lens is the focal length.

Use your light rays kit to measure the focal length of some of your cylindrical lenses. You will have to invent a way of producing parallel rays of light.

Physicists often measure the *power* of a lens rather than its focal length:

$$\text{power} = \frac{1}{\text{focal length}}.$$

If the focal length is in metres, then the power is in **dioptres**. For example, a lens of

105

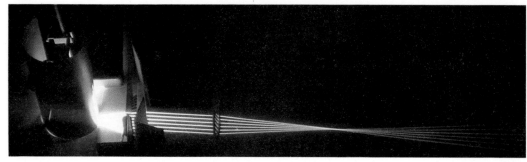

Fig. 6.41   Using the light rays kit to find the focal length of a cylindrical lens

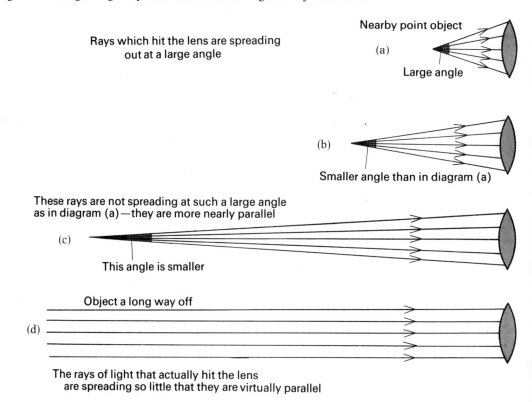

Nearby point object

(a)

Rays which hit the lens are spreading out at a large angle

Large angle

(b)

Smaller angle than in diagram (a)

These rays are not spreading at such a large angle as in diagram (a)—they are more nearly parallel

(c)

This angle is smaller

Object a long way off

(d)

The rays of light that actually hit the lens are spreading so little that they are virtually parallel

Fig. 6.42   Why rays of light from a distant object are almost parallel

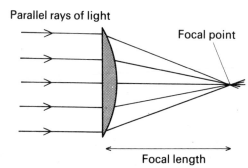

Parallel rays of light

Focal point

Focal length

focal length 2 m has a power of $\frac{1}{2}$ dioptre. A lens with a focal length $\frac{1}{4}$ metre has a power of 4 dioptres. If you wear spectacles the optician will have used dioptres on the prescription for your lenses.

Work out the power of all the lenses whose focal length you have measured.

Fig. 6.43   The focal length of a lens

6.14 The magnifying glass

You must have used your lens in the way that Jillian is doing in Fig. 6.44—as a magnifying glass. If not, then it is time you did. Look at the image through a magnifying glass like the one in Fig. 6.45. In what way is it *different* from the image made with the same lens when it was used in the lens camera?

Fig. 6.44 Jillian using a lens as a magnifying glass to study a map. Notice how close her eye is to the lens

Fig. 6.45 The image of the map seen through the magnifying glass. Is this in any way different to the image made by your camera?

How close can you put your eye to the magnifying glass and still see the image? That's right—right next to the lens, as Jillian is doing. Where, then, is the image? There is no room for it between your eye and the lens, and even if there were, you would not be able to see it since it would be nearer your eye than your near point. Yet you are certainly looking at an image with this lens. So it must be on the same side of the lens as the object that it is magnifying, which is very strange! The light rays kit can tell you how this happens.

Using just one lamp, set up your light rays kit in the usual way. A magnifying glass goes very close to the object it is magnifying, so put the convex lens close to the lamp as in Fig. 6.46. The lens is so close to the lamp that it cannot bend the rays sufficiently to bring them together to form an image. They are still spreading out (but not as much as before). If an eye is behind the lens, it will intercept these rays of light as in Fig. 6.47. As far as the eye is concerned, the rays of light are *behaving as if* they are coming from the point shown in Fig. 6.47. This is the image your eye sees through a magnifying glass. The rays of light do not really go through this point, but behave as if they are coming from there. It is called a **virtual image**. You cannot catch this image on a piece of paper, unlike the other images you had with a convex lens. Images which can be formed on a piece of paper are called **real images**.

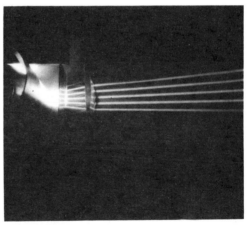

Fig. 6.46 Using the light rays kit to investigate how a magnifying glass works

Although Fig. 6.47 shows you how a magnifying glass makes a virtual image, it does not tell you anything about why the virtual image is *bigger* than the original object. To investigate this, you need two lamps, to represent the top and

107

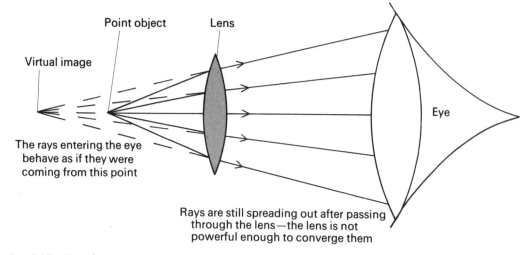

Fig. 6.47   How the eye sees a virtual image

bottom of the object in the same way as you did in Section 6.12.

Fig. 6.48 shows a suitable arrangement of the apparatus and shows what happens to the rays of light. Set this arrangement up for yourself. Try to find out how to obtain the biggest magnification.

Can you find a rule, as you did in Section 6.12, connecting the magnification, the image distance and the object distance?

Copy out the following paragraph, using the correct alternatives, as a

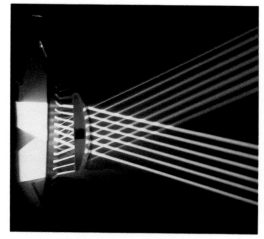

Fig. 6.48   Investigating the size of a virtual image using the light rays kit

Fig. 6.49   Ray diagram showing how an 'extended' virtual image is formed

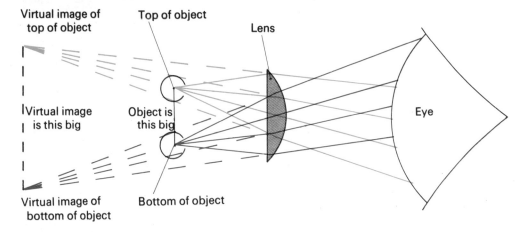

108

summary of what you have learned about real and virtual images.

'A convex lens can be used to make a real image on a screen. The image is *upside-down/the right way up* and is on the *same/opposite* side of the lens *as/to* the object. The image is *bigger/smaller/can be bigger or smaller* than the object. A convex lens can also be used as a magnifying glass, when the image *is bigger/is smaller/ can be bigger or smaller* than the object, and is *upside-down/the right way up*. The image is on the *same side/opposite side* of the lens *as/to* the object, and is said to be a *real/virtual* image.'

6.15 The astronomical telescope

The largest and most imposing optical instruments are undoubtedly the telescopes used by astronomers. Some idea of the size of a really large telescope can be gained from Fig. 6.50.

Fig. 6.51   A view of the Triffid Nebula through the 48 inch telescope of the Royal Observatory, Edinburgh

There are several different sorts of telescope. You are going to make a model of the kind invented by Johannes Kepler in the 1620s. This was not the first kind of telescope to be designed. Nobody is really sure who invented the first telescope, (the **terrestrial telescope**) but it is thought that a Dutch lens maker called Hans Lippershey discovered it by accident in about 1608. Galileo heard of it, copied and improved it.

A simple model of Kepler's **astronomical telescope** is being used by Paul in Fig. 6.52. The two lenses which are used in this telescope are mounted in wooden holders fixed to a steel bar.

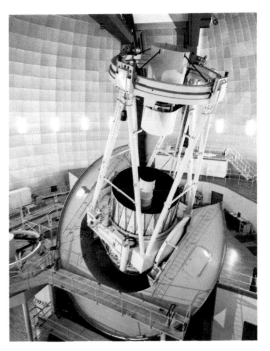

Fig. 6.50   The Anglo-Australian telescope. Notice how it dwarfs the person standing next to it

Fig. 6.52   Paul using a simple astronomical telescope (but he's not looking at stars!)   109

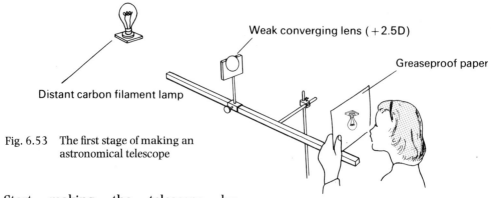

Weak converging lens (+2.5D)

Greaseproof paper

Distant carbon filament lamp

Fig. 6.53 The first stage of making an astronomical telescope

Start making the telescope by mounting a weak convex lens (about 2.5 dioptres) at one end of the bar. Point this lens at a distant lamp and use a piece of greaseproof paper to find the real image of this lamp, as in Fig. 6.53.

Next mount a strong convex lens (say 14 dioptres) a little nearer to you than the image you have just found, as in the next diagram. This strong lens acts as a magnifying glass and magnifies the real image formed by the first lens. Focus the magnifying glass on the image that you can see on the greaseproof paper.

Take away the piece of greaseproof paper and look carefully through the magnifying glass. You may have to alter slightly the position of the magnifying glass to get the best view. Does the lamp look bigger or smaller than without the telescope? (If it is smaller, you have made a mistake!)

The lamp is upside-down. Why? Shouldn't the image through a magnifying glass be the right way up?

The weak lens nearer the lamp is called the **objective lens**; the magnifying glass is called the **eyepiece lens**.

This sort of telescope is called an astronomical telescope and is used for looking at stars and planets.

Why do you think this telescope is satisfactory for looking at stars and planets but is inconvenient for looking at ships on the sea, or people out of the window?

To make a *powerful* telescope a *weak* objective lens and a *strong* eyepiece is needed. Since a weak objective lens will make a real image a long way from the lens, a powerful telescope will be a very *long* instrument. But there is another very important point about telescopes. Many stars are far too faint to be seen by your naked eye; not enough light gets into the eye. A telescope with a *wide* objective lens allows an astronomer to see faint stars that he would not be able to see otherwise. How does a large objective lens allow this to happen?

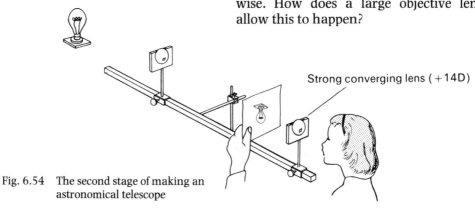

Strong converging lens (+14D)

Fig. 6.54 The second stage of making an astronomical telescope

Fig. 6.55 The Yerkes Observatory telescope—the world's largest refracting telescope—the sort Paul is using in Fig. 6.52

The telescope which you made is a **refracting** telescope. The Yerkes observatory in Wisconsin, USA has the largest astronomical refracting telescope in the world. The objective lens is 1 metre wide. How much more light will enter this telescope than your naked eye?

An even larger objective lens would collect even more light, but problems arise. It would be very difficult to make a large lens accurately, and it would sag under its own weight (it cannot be supported underneath!) Bigger telescopes, like the Anglo-Australian telescope in Fig. 6.50, use a special concave mirror to make the first real image. Such a telescope is called a **reflecting** telescope, and was invented by Sir Isaac Newton in 1671.

As a challenge to you, see if you can set up a ray model of the refracting, astronomical telescope using the light rays kit.

Fig. 6.56 How a reflecting telescope works

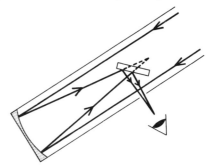

Remember that it is for looking at *distant* objects, so the lamps in your kit must be a long way from the objective lens.

6.16 The microscope

Fig. 6.57 An early microscope

A microscope was invented in 1590, some years before the telescope. It uses the same system of lenses as an astronomical telescope, but since the object is very close to the objective lens, this lens has to be a powerful lens so that a real image is formed for the eyepiece to magnify. Fig. 6.58 shows the general arrangement of a microscope.

Try to set up a model microscope in the same way as you set up a model telescope in the last section. Your object will need to be mounted fairly close to the strong objective lens. A small picture drawn on a piece of paper would do.

111

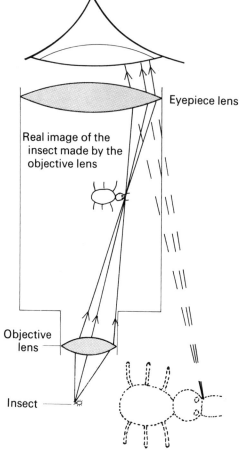

Eyepiece lens

Real image of the insect made by the objective lens

Objective lens

Insect

Enlarged virtual image made by the eyepiece lens

Fig. 6.58　How a microscope makes a large image

You learned earlier in the chapter that strong lenses cause distorted images (the distortions are called **aberrations**). Since the objective lens is a strong one, designing a distortion-free objective lens is difficult. An objective lens in a microscope will consist of a combination of several lenses in the same way as the lens of a high quality camera.

Why do you think that specimens under a microscope have to be strongly illuminated, especially at high magnifications?

6.17　Mirrors and periscopes

You must have done what Beatrice is doing in Fig. 6.59 many times. Where is

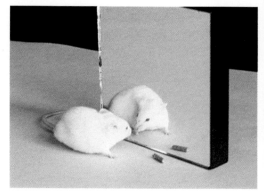

Fig. 6.59　Where is Beatrice's image?

Beatrice's image? Where is your image? How *far* is it behind the mirror?

Do you think that it is a real image? (Do the rays of light really go through the image behind the mirror?) Or is it a virtual image?

Is there any rule about the way in which a mirror reflects rays of light? Design an experiment to find out, using apparatus as in Fig. 6.60. Draw a diagram to show how to set up the apparatus, explain what you do and make a table of any readings you take. Can you find a rule?

Fig. 6.60　Design an experiment using this apparatus to find a rule about the way in which mirrors reflect rays of light

How can you use one mirror, by itself, to see round an awkward corner of a road, as in the plan in Fig. 6.61? Copy the diagram and mark where and how you would place the mirror to help the car driver see round the sharp corner.

Now use two mirrors, and whatever

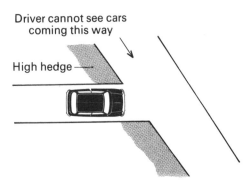

Fig. 6.61   Where would you put a mirror to help the car driver see what is coming down the road?

Fig. 6.62   Why are they using periscopes?

else you need, to design and build a **periscope**.

Why are the people in Fig. 6.62 using periscopes? Where else might you find a periscope?

6.18   Curved mirrors

Not all mirrors are flat like those with which you made a periscope. Some are curved. Convex mirrors curve towards you. Look into one. What does your image look like? How big is it? Which way up is it?

Fig. 6.63 shows the view through a convex mirror used as a rear-view mirror on a car. Can you think of any *advantage* in using a convex mirror here. What *disadvantages* are there?

A concave mirror curves the other way. Hold a concave mirror at arm's length and look at it. What does your

Fig. 6.63   View through a convex mirror on a car

image look like? What happens as you bring the mirror closer to you? Can you think of a use for a concave mirror?

6.19   Bending light

There is something a little odd about the pen in Fig. 6.64, isn't there? Is it a trick pen, or does yours do the same thing?

Fig. 6.64   Is this a trick pen?

Here is another little experiment. Put a penny in the bottom of a tin can or cup (but not something with transparent sides). Stand the can on the bench and then stand back from the bench so you just cannot see the penny (Fig. 6.65). Do not move. Ask a friend to fill the can slowly with water from a beaker without disturbing the penny. What happens?

Next time you are at a swimming pool or by a clear pond or river, notice how the water seems shallower than it really is.

113

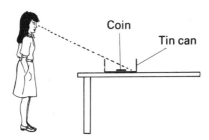

Stand where you just cannot see the coin

Fig. 6.65

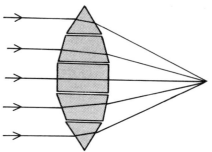

Each bit of the lens behaves as if it were a part of a prism

Light bends (or 'refracts') at each surface

Fig. 6.67　Why a convex lens converges light

How can you explain these facts? You will need to know what water does to rays of light.

Fig. 6.66 shows a ray of light passing through a box of water; the box is painted white on the bottom. Notice what is happening to the light as it goes into and comes out of the water. Set up this apparatus for yourself and try twisting the box around. Does the ray do anything else?

Fig. 6.66　A ray of light passing through a container of water

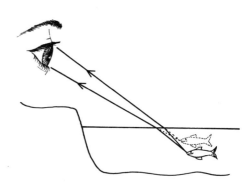

Fig. 6.68　The fish is not where it seems to be!

6.20　Further work

Although you have looked at quite a variety of optical instruments and learned a little of what lenses and mirrors can do to rays of light, there is much you have *not* looked at. You might like to investigate some other things for yourself. For example:

1 Use a light rays kit to find out how curved mirrors make images. Try to draw ray diagrams like the one in Fig. 6.39.

2 Find out about what prisms do to rays of light.

3 How does a *terrestrial* telescope work? (The eyepiece is a concave lens.)

The bending of a ray of light in this way is called **refraction**.

Notice which way the light bends. It is refraction that makes a lens bend rays of light so that they can be focused. Fig. 6.67 illustrates this.

Fig. 6.68 shows why the bending of light rays makes things in water seem less deep than they really are.

_____SUMMARY_____

Now that you have finished studying this chapter on optical instruments, there are a number of things that you should know or be able to do.

1 You should:
  a) know that rays of light travel in straight lines;
  b) know how to make a pinhole camera;
  c) be able to explain why the image in a pinhole camera is upside-down;
  d) be able to predict the size of the image in a pinhole camera;
  e) be able to make a simple lens camera, and explain how it works;
  f) know how a lens forms a real image, and how it forms a virtual image;
  g) know the differences between a real and a virtual image;
  h) know the factors affecting the sharpness of a photograph;
  i) be able to make an astronomical telescope, and explain how it works;
  j) be able to explain why a telescope makes things appear brighter;
  k) know what is meant by the magnification produced by a lens;
  l) know about the structure of the eye;
  m) know some of the defects of vision that can occur;
  n) be able to make a periscope;
  o) be able to use a light rays kit to find out how rays of light behave.
  p) know what is meant by refraction of light.
  q) know that the power of a lens is 1/focal length.

2 You should know what each of the following is, or what it does:

optics
optical instrument
image
convex lens
concave lens
ray diagram
smoke box
focusing
focal length
focal point
shutter
aperture
retina
optic nerve

cornea
ciliary muscles
iris
blind spot
range of
  accommodation
near point
far point
long sight
short sight
objective lens
eyepiece lens
aberration
dioptre

3 These are some of the other words that have been used in this chapter. You should know what they mean:

simplification
adequate
dissect
concentrate
interpret

transparent
distort
exposure
structure

_____FURTHER QUESTIONS_____

1 The lamp shown in Fig. 6.69 is 10 cm tall. It is placed 20 cm in front of a pinhole camera; the camera itself is 20 cm long.
  a) How big is the image of the lamp?
  b) How big would the image be if the lamp were 120 cm away from the pinhole?
  c) How big would the image be if the lamp were 2 cm away from the pinhole?
  d) What difference would it make

to your answers to the above questions if a lens were placed in front of the pinhole?

2 Find five photographs in this book which were probably taken with a fast shutter speed. Say why you think a fast shutter speed was used.

3 Find five photographs in this book which were probably taken with a small aperture. Say why you think a small aperture was used.

4 Why does it not matter that a lens   115

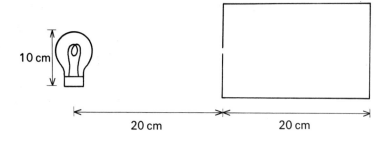

Fig. 6.69

camera takes a photograph that is upside-down?

5 a) What is the power of a lens of focal length $+\frac{1}{4}$ m?

b) What is the power of a lens of focal length -20 cm?

c) What is the focal length of a lens of power $-\frac{1}{8}$ dioptre?

d) What is the focal length of a lens of power 2 dioptres? In each case, say whether the lens is a convex or concave lens.

6 An eye and a camera are similar in some ways, and different in others. Write down all the similarities you can think of between an eye and a camera, and then write down all the differences you can think of.

7 Many animals, especially smaller animals like birds, have their eyes in the sides of their heads, while other animals, including you, have eyes in the front of their heads. Why do you think it might be useful to have eyes in the sides of your head. What are the advantages of having eyes in the front of your head?

8 Some people (especially older people) wear **bifocal lenses**—lenses which are divided into two parts. The top part has one focal length and the bottom part has another focal length. They can use the same spectacles to see both near and far objects distinctly.

a) Which part of the lens do you think is for seeing near objects, like a newspaper? The top or the bottom part?

b) What can you deduce about the range of accommodation of these people?

9 Fig. 6.70 shows an object 10 cm high placed 50 cm from a convex lens. An image is formed 150 cm beyond the lens, as shown.

a) Which way up is the image?

b) How tall is the image?

c) Copy the diagram and draw a cone of rays from the top of the object, passing through the lens and con-

Fig. 6.70

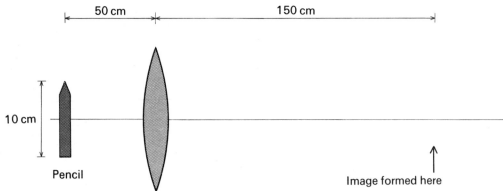

verging at the correct spot on the image.

d) Draw an eye in an appropriate place on your diagram. Draw your rays continuing on into the eye to show how the eye sees the image.

10 Fig. 6.71 shows some rays of light passing through some boxes. There is a lens in each box.

a) Which box has the most powerful lens?

b) Which box has the weakest lens?

c) Which boxes have concave lenses?

d) Which boxes have convex lenses?

e) Which box has the lens most suitable for a magnifying glass?

f) Which box has the lens most suitable for the objective lens of an astronomical telescope?

g) Which box has the lens most suitable for the objective lens of a microscope?

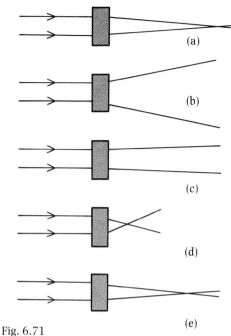

Fig. 6.71

117

7

WAVES WAVES WAVES

Fig. 7.1   Mike's becalmed sailing boat

7.1   Introduction

A problem for Mike—how to get his becalmed sailing ship in the photograph back to dry land. This is also a practical physics problem! To put the problem in terms of physics, how can he give his boat some kinetic energy so that it moves. Not wanting to get his feet wet, he threw some stones at the boat, but missed! But the ship *did* start moving—mostly bobbing up and down, but nevertheless this showed some energy *was* reaching the ship. How did it get there if the stones were not touching the ship?

When a stone falls into water, a little group of **water waves** spreads out, as in Fig. 7.2. These waves carry energy. Big

Fig. 7.2   A group of water waves spreading out

waves carry a lot of energy, which can cause considerable destruction, as Fig. 7.3 reminds you. There has been some research into the possibility of using the energy of water waves to generate electrical energy (Fig. 7.4).

Fig. 7.3   Waves can carry a lot of energy

There are other sorts of waves apart from water waves. Many different sorts of energy are carried by different waves. Sound is carried by waves, so is light, so are radio and television signals. How do we know? To answer this question you must first find out a little about what a wave *is* and what it *does*.

7.2   Waves on springs

Stretch out a 'Slinky' or similar spring on the floor, with someone holding it at each end as in Fig. 7.5. (The photograph in Fig. 7.5 was actually taken outdoors—can you think why?) One person should send one wave down the spring with a quick

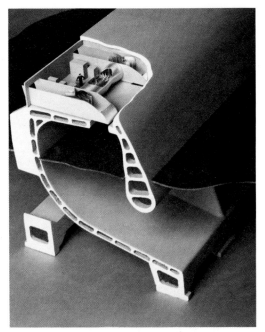

Fig. 7.4   A model of a 'wave piston' for generating electricity

flick of the wrist. Notice that for any point on the spring, after the wave passes the spring returns to exactly where it was before. This is very important. Although the spring is transferring energy, in the form of a wave, from one end to the other, the spring itself does not end up in a different place. The same applies to ripples on the lake in Fig. 7.2. When the waves have finished spreading out, there is *not* a pile of water round the edge of the lake and a hole in the middle!

Look at the *direction* in which the individual coils of the spring in Fig. 7.5 move. They move *across*, at right angles to, the way in which the wave is moving.

Fig. 7.5   Making a wave on a long spring

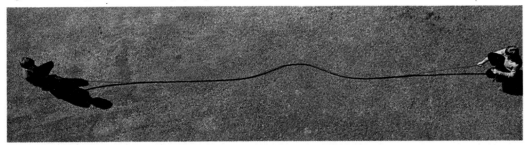

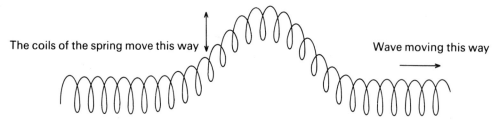

The coils of the spring move this way ↓   Wave moving this way →

Fig. 7.6   A transverse wave

Fig. 7.6 illustrates this point. A wave like this is called a **transverse wave**.

A different sort of wave can be shown by holding a slightly stretched Slinky spring as Fiona is doing in Fig. 7.7. Someone will have to anchor the bottom in

Fig. 7.7   Making a longitudinal wave

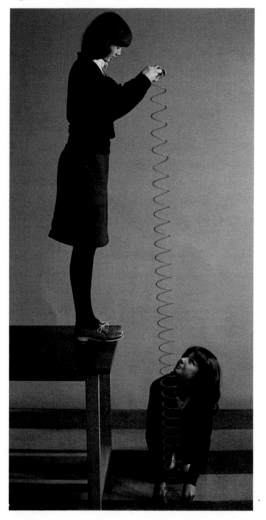

Wave moving this way ↓

Coils of spring moving this way, in the same direction as the wave ↕

Fig. 7.8   A longitudinal wave

the way Jillian is doing. Move the top of the spring sharply down then up. (This is not easy—you will need to practice.) The two people at the top and bottom of the spring will not see much, but anyone looking from where the photograph was taken should see a wave travelling down (and probably reflected back up) the spring. This time the coils of the spring move as in Fig. 7.8. This sort of wave is called a **longitudinal wave**.

The last paragraph mentioned the possibility of a wave reflecting. Did the transverse wave in Fig. 7.5 reflect when it got to the end? If so, does it go on bouncing backwards and forwards for ever?

If you roll two marbles towards each other they bounce off each other. Does the same happen to waves? Send out a wave from each end of the spring at the same time. What happens when they meet? Do they bounce off each other, just stop, or what? You will probably have to design and carry out a few experiments before you can be absolutely sure about the answer to this question.

7.3 Water waves

What sort of waves are water waves—transverse or longitudinal? Since the surface of the water goes up and down, transverse would seem to be a reasonable answer. But it is not quite as simple as that. Water waves normally travel too fast for you to be able to see easily what is happening, but they can be slowed down by pouring a layer of paraffin on top of the water. If you do this in a deep, clear tank like the one illustrated in Fig. 7.9, then you can see the waves from the side. Weigh down a cork with a drawing pin and Plasticine until it floats on the surface of the *water*. This allows you to see the way the water moves. After the liquid in the tank has become still, send one wave along with a plunger. Can you work out which way the water is moving?

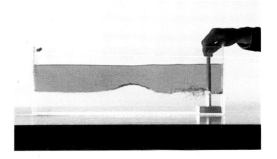

Fig. 7.9   A side view of a water wave in a tank. The paraffin on top of the water slows down the wave

7.4 The ripple tank

To find out more about waves it is useful to look at waves that can spread out, like the waves on the lake at the beginning of this chapter. Waves on a spring obviously cannot do this! Water waves are the most sensible choice for study since you can actually *see* them, but a lake would hardly be a sensible place to choose to start to investigate water waves, even if there is one near your school. (Why not?)

Fig. 7.10 shows a suitable laboratory apparatus for investigating water waves. It is called a **ripple tank**. (A ripple is a little wave.) There is a hole at the bottom of the tank so that the tank can be emptied. Seal this hole with a cork then half fill the tank with water. Use a beaker to fill the tank; do not try to carry the tank to a tap.

Fig. 7.10   A ripple tank—for investigating waves

It is not easy to see ripples on the water; the photograph of the apparatus shows a lamp that can be used so that the ripples show up as shadows on the white paper underneath the tank. Adjust the lamp so the filament is horizontal to get the best shadows on the paper.

It is best to put the tank on the lab floor, not on a bench, which usually vibrates too much and so causes odd waves all over the tank. Even on the floor the tank may suffer from these vibrations. Your tank should have a sloping 'beach' round

121

the side—running your finger round this 'beach' to wet it helps to damp out stray waves. In really bad cases you may have to stand the feet of your tank on little pads of foam rubber.

7.5 Reflection of waves

You already know that waves can be reflected. (How do you know?) Start using your ripple tank by investigating this a little further.

Put a straight barrier across one end of your ripple tank as in Fig. 7.11 and make a circular, spreading wave in the middle of your tank by gently dipping your finger into the water.

Fig. 7.11   A straight barrier for reflecting waves

1 What is the shape of the wave when it has rebounded from the barrier?
2 Does it matter how close to the barrier you start the wave?
3 Where does the reflecting wave behave as if it were spreading from?
4 Does the wave stay the same *strength* all the time?
5 Can you change the *speed* of the wave? Now use a *straight* wave instead of a circular wave. This is best made with a wooden rod or ruler, or other straight object, as in Fig. 7.12. Just roll the rod forward slightly—you are not trying to make a tidal wave! This may need a little practice.

Fig. 7.12   One way of making a straight wave

You can arrange your barrier 'square on' to the oncoming waves (Fig. 7.13) or at an angle to them, as in the next diagram. There are lots of angles to try!

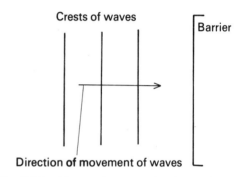

Fig. 7.13   A barrier 'square on' to the oncoming waves

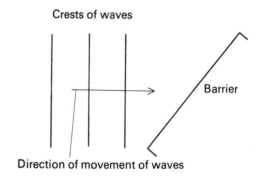

Fig. 7.14   A barrier at an angle to the oncoming waves

Can you find a *rule* connecting the direction in which a straight wave is reflected from a barrier and the direction in which it hits the barrier? Write down what you discover, with a diagram to make it clear. (*Caution:* make sure the barrier itself does not vibrate and send out its own waves.)

122

As well as a straight barrier to reflect your waves, you could use a *curved* barrier, such as in Fig. 7.15. If you have time, try reflecting waves off a curved barrier. Remember that you could place your barrier either way round, and that you could use either straight or circular waves. Draw diagrams showing what happens to your waves after they leave the barrier.

Fig. 7.16   A vibrator, for sending out a continuous stream of waves

Fig. 7.15   What does a curved barrier do to waves?

7.6   Continuous waves

Fig. 7.17   Sphere on a vibrator for making circular waves

So far you have used short **pulses** of waves in your investigation of reflection. Sometimes it is more convenient to use many waves one after the other—continuous waves. To make these, you *could* keep dipping your finger in the water or keep rolling your ruler backwards and forwards, but this would be tedious and the waves would not be very regular.

Fig. 7.16 shows an addition to a ripple tank—a vibrator. This is designed to send out continuous waves for you. The motor has a wheel on the shaft that is mounted off-centre, so that as the motor goes round it wobbles the wooden beam.

If you want straight waves the wooden beam should *just* be in the water. To get circular waves raise the beam a little and lower one of the spheres into the water (Fig. 7.17).

The motor on your vibrator is probably a direct-current motor working off a maximum of 4 to 5 volts. You are less likely to burn out your motor if you use batteries to power it. You can change the motor speed by changing the number of batteries you use. If this does not provide a fine enough control of the speed, then you could include a variable resistor in the circuit.

Use your vibrator to send straight waves across the tank. Even at a low motor speed you will probably find a snag very soon—you cannot see them! There are too many waves leaving the vibrator every second (the 'frequency' is too high) for you to be able to distinguish the individual waves. How do you overcome this problem?

123

7.7 Stroboscopes

The trick is to 'freeze' the waves—make them *appear* to stand still. This is done with a stroboscope such as Mike is using in Fig. 7.18. You have already met one sort of **stroboscope** before, the flashing light shown in Fig. 4.20. This is a different sort of stroboscope. It is a disc with slots cut in it. The disc can be turned on its handle using the finger hole. You look through the slits. How does it work?

Fig. 7.18   Mike using a stroboscope

Use your stroboscope to look at a turning wheel on which there is an arrow—Fig. 7.19. If you turn your stroboscope at just the right speed so that each slit appears opposite your eye when the arrow is, say, upright, you will just

Fig. 7.19   Can you use a stroboscope to make the turning arrow appear to be still?

catch glimpses of the arrow when it is upright and the wheel will appear not to move.

You can, of course, achieve the same effect with the flashing light stroboscope from Chapter 4, arranging it to flash once for every revolution of the wheel.

What happens if you turn your stroboscope a little too fast or a little too slow? Suppose you turn your stroboscope at *twice* the speed you need to 'freeze' the motion. Write down what you see.

Try looking through your stroboscope at the continuous waves on your ripple tank. You might also like to try using your stroboscope in the way that Fiona is doing in Fig. 7.20, turning it in front of the lamp to give the effect of a flashing lamp. This might make the light too faint to be useful, though. With a little practice, you should be able to make the waves appear stationary.

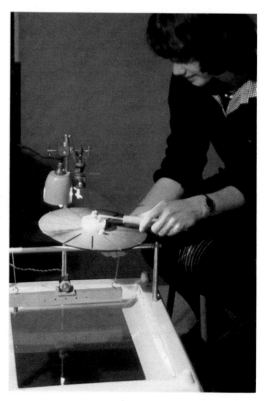

Fig. 7.20   An alternative way of using a stroboscope

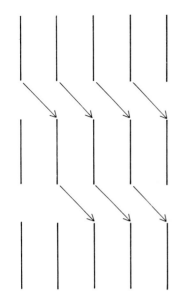

Position of wave crests at one 'glimpse' of the waves through the stroboscope

At the next glimpse, each wave has moved on one place, into the place occupied by its neighbour

At the next glimpse, each wave has moved on one more place

Fig. 7.21   Why waves viewed through a stroboscope appear to be still, provided the stroboscope is turning at the right speed

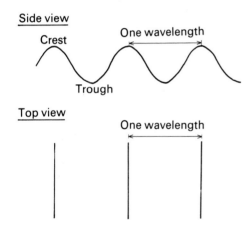

Positions of crests of waves
Each line represents the crest of a wave

Fig. 7.22   The wavelength of a wave

With your waves 'frozen', you should be able to see that there is a definite distance between the crest of each wave. This distance is called the **wavelength** of the waves.

The number of waves sent out every second by the vibrator is called the **frequency** of the waves. This is measured in **hertz**; 1 hertz is 1 wave every second.

What happens to the wavelength of your waves if you make the motor turn faster so that the frequency increases?

7.8   Refraction of waves

In very shallow water, waves travel more slowly than in deep water. If waves reach a boundary between deep and shallow water at an angle as in Fig. 7.23, then one end of the wave will reach the shallow water first and slow down before the other end. This will slew the wave

Fig. 7.23   Refraction of waves

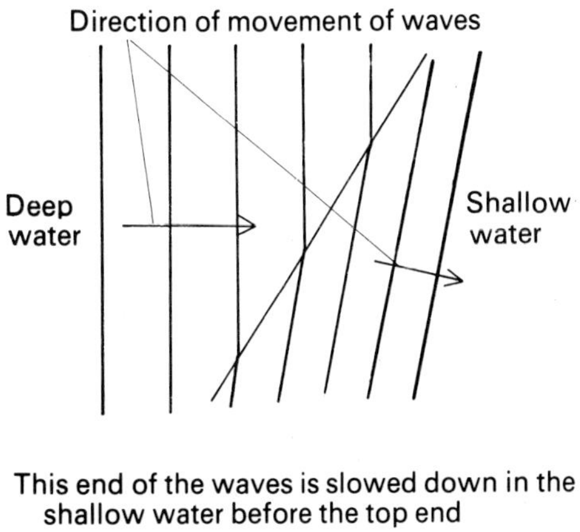

Direction of movement of waves

Deep water · Shallow water

This end of the waves is slowed down in the shallow water before the top end

125

round so that it travels in a new direction. This changing of direction is called **refraction**.

You have already met the idea of refraction elsewhere in this book. Where?

Can you work out what will happen to the wavelength of the wave in the shallow water?

Use a piece of glass to make a shallow area in your ripple tank, and see if you can find any signs of refraction of water waves. (The shallow area of water must be *very* shallow.)

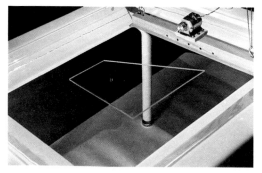

Fig. 7.24   Making a shallow area in your ripple tank

7.9   Sending waves through gaps

Something very interesting happens when a wave goes through a hole, or a gap, in a barrier. A gap can easily be made between two straight reflectors as in Fig. 7.25. The next photograph shows what happened on one occasion when waves went through such a gap—they

Fig. 7.25   A gap in a barrier. What happens as the waves go through?

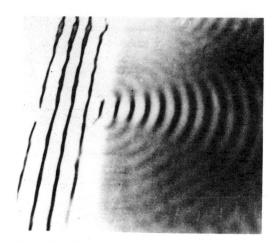

Fig. 7.26   Waves going through a gap

tend to spread out a little behind the barrier. This is called **diffraction**. Do your water waves diffract when they go through a gap? Does it matter how wide the gap is? Try a very wide and a very narrow gap. (Wide and narrow compared to what?)

Only waves diffract. Solid objects like footballs do not diffract. Just imagine the football in Fig. 7.27 spreading out as it goes through the goalmouth! This is one way of deciding whether something consists of waves or particles. Waves diffract, and particles do not. The next section looks at something else that only waves do.

Fig. 7.27   Will this football diffract as it goes through the goal mouth?

7.10 Adding waves together

You need to use circular waves for this experiment, so adjust the height of your vibrator so that the circular wave makers just touch the water. Use two circular wave makers, side by side, as in Fig. 7.28 so that, when you switch on the motor, two identical sets of waves will travel down your ripple tank. Obviously, they will overlap as they spread down the tank. What happens when they overlap. Look at Fig. 7.29. This photograph shows two sets of overlapping waves, and you can see that there are some paths along the tank where there *are* waves, and other paths where there are no waves.

Fig. 7.29 Overlapping waves from two vibrators

Fig. 7.28 Two circular wave makers

Try to obtain this pattern with your tank. Does changing the wavelength change the pattern? Suppose you use two wave makers that are further apart. Does this make any difference to the pattern?

This pattern needs explaining. How can two sets of waves join together to give places where there are no waves at all?

Remember that water waves consist of crests and troughs following each other. Suppose, at some place in your tank, a crest from one vibrator arrived at the same time as a crest from the other vibrator. These two crests would pile one

Fig. 7.30 Explaining interference

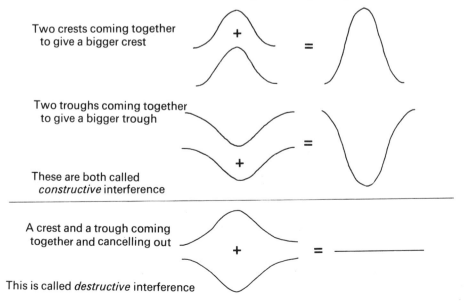

Two crests coming together to give a bigger crest

Two troughs coming together to give a bigger trough

These are both called *constructive* interference

A crest and a trough coming together and cancelling out

This is called *destructive* interference

127

on top of the other and form a bigger crest as in Fig. 7.30. A small time later a trough will arrive from one rippler at the same time as a trough from the other rippler. These will add together to give an even deeper trough.

The waves from one rippler are adding to and reinforcing the waves from the other rippler. Physicists call this **constructive interference** of waves.

In another part of the tank, a crest from one rippler might arrive at the same time as the trough from the other one. The crest will 'fill in' the trough. The waves will cancel and give flat water. This is called **destructive interference**.

Fig. 7.31 explains how the pattern over a large area of your ripple tank occurs. This pattern that you have seen is called an **interference pattern**.

Only waves interfere. Particles do not. Can you imagine one billiard ball hitting another billiard ball and both of them cancelling out, giving no billiard ball? What about one hockey ball hitting another one to make a hockey ball twice as big?

7.11 Summary of the way waves behave

Fill in the missing words in the following paragraph. To make a change from other similar paragraphs in this book, there is no list of words from which to choose!

'There are *four* things that waves can do. They can bounce off a barrier. This is called _____. The angle at which straight waves hit a straight barrier _____ the angle at which the waves leave the barrier. Circular waves come back from the barrier in a _____ shape, behaving as if they were coming from _____.

Waves can also change direction. This is called _____. It happens when waves change their speed. When a wave slows down, the _____ also gets smaller.

When a wave goes through a gap in a barrier, it might _____. This is called _____. The effect is most noticeable if the gap is of _____ width to the wavelength, when the waves emerge in a _____ shape, whatever

Fig. 7.31 Explaining the interference pattern in Fig. 7.29

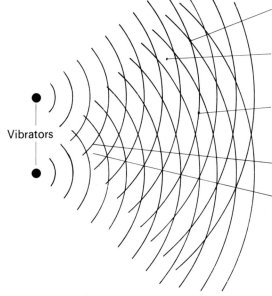

Vibrators

Here, a crest from one vibrator is meeting a crest from the other vibrator to give a big crest

Here, a trough from one vibrator is meeting a trough from the other vibrator to give a big trough

Here, a crest from one vibrator is meeting a trough from the other vibrator to give no wave

Along this line, crests and troughs are always cancelling to give no wave

Along this line, crests from each vibrator arrive together, and troughs from each vibrator arrive together, resulting in a big wave

the shape was before they came to the gap.

Waves can also combine together, either constructively or destructively. This is called _____.

Only waves can _____ and _____.

7.12   Other waves

At the start of this chapter it was mentioned that sound and light are carried by waves. This can only be true if they behave like water waves. In particular, since *only* waves will interfere or diffract, then you must look for interference or diffraction of sound or light to show they are waves. It is usually easier to look for interference.

7.13   Interference of sound

Put two loudspeakers about a metre apart and connect them to an **oscillator** as in the photograph. An oscillator causes the speaker to give only a single musical note. Set the oscillator to a frequency of about 500 Hz and stand 2 m away from the speakers. Walk across in front of the speakers. What do you hear? What can you deduce from what you hear?

Suppose you use a higher or a lower frequency. Does this make any difference to what you hear as you walk across in front of the speakers? Can you explain any difference you hear?

7.14   Radar waves

The **radar waves** given out by the transmitter illustrated in Fig. 7.33 are often called **microwaves**. If they really are waves, they should diffract as they go through the gap in the barrier in Fig. 7.34.

Fig. 7.33   Does this give out waves?

Fig. 7.32   An oscillator connected to two loudspeakers. Do the sound waves interfere?

Fig. 7.34 Searching for diffraction of microwaves

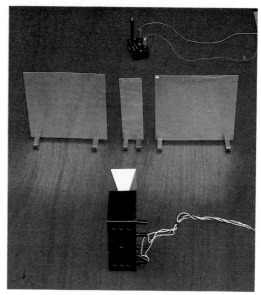

Fig. 7.35 Searching for interference of microwaves

The detector shown in the photograph is connected to an amplifier and loudspeaker. Between them they convert the microwave energy into sound energy so you can use your ears to listen for the microwaves.

When you use this apparatus, is there any evidence that the microwaves are spreading out as they pass through the gap? Are the microwaves really waves?

As well as looking for diffraction, you could look for interference. To do this, you need two sources of these waves. Here is a problem. It is unlikely that your school will have two transmitters, and even if it does, it is very unlikely that the two transmitters will send out absolutely identical waves.

Fig. 7.35 shows a way round this problem, which only works if the microwaves diffract as they go through a gap. If you found that they did not diffract, then this suggestion will not work and you will have to think of something else. If you arrange two slits about 10 cm apart a little way in front of one transmitter, then as the waves go through each of the slits and spread out, they will overlap and so interfere.

Assemble the apparatus as shown in the photograph and slide the detector across the bench behind the slits. Do you find any evidence for interference? Are there any places where the waves are cancelling out? Is this in any way similar to what you heard when listening for interference of sound waves?

7.15 Light waves

Everyday experience should suggest to you that light does *not* consist of waves. Light is not seen to spread out as it comes in through a window. If there are two lamps on in a room, there are not places where light from one lamp cancels light from the other lamp, leaving dark patches in the room. Why, then, do physicists talk of light waves?

Remember that, when you looked at water waves diffracting, they only diffracted noticeably when the gap was about the same size as the wavelength of the waves. Perhaps the window is too big a gap to show diffraction of light? Perhaps the wavelength of light is very small, and you are going to have to look very carefully for evidence that light is waves.

Start by looking for diffraction. You need a very narrow slit—less than $\frac{1}{2}$ millimetre wide. You could try painting a microscope slide with black paint and then, when the paint is dry, ruling a line through the paint using a razor blade or a very sharp knife. Or you could put the two halves of a broken razor blade between two pieces of card with a hole in it as in Fig. 7.36. You can make a narrow slit between the two straight edges of the razor blade.

Fig. 7.37   A lamp with a simple vertical filament

Fig. 7.36   How to make a narrow slit

Put the slit close to your eye and look through it at a lamp that is 2–3 metres away. A lamp with a simple vertical filament, like in Fig. 7.37, is best. Do you see any evidence that light is diffracting? Is it diffracting very much?

You could look for interference of light using a similar arrangement of apparatus to that which you used for microwaves (Fig. 7.34) but with the dimensions changed to suit the very small wavelength which you think light waves have.

Fig. 7.38 shows a diagram of suitable apparatus, while the next photograph shows a way of setting it out on the bench. The lens concentrates the light on to the screen to make it easier to see if there is any interference. It should be a weak lens—about 2 dioptres.

Fig. 7.38   Apparatus with which to look for the interference of light

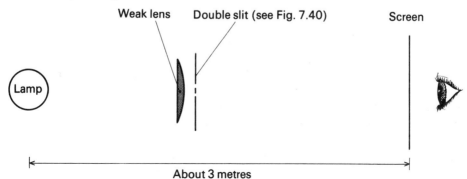

Weak lens   Double slit (see Fig. 7.40)   Screen

Lamp

About 3 metres

131

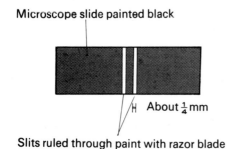

Fig. 7.39   The apparatus of
Fig. 7.38 laid out on a bench

To set up the apparatus, put a lamp at one end of a bench and the screen about 4 metres away. Move the lens between the lamp and the screen until you get a large, sharp image of the lamp filament on the screen. (There will probably be two positions of the lens where you obtain an image of the filament. One of these positions gives a small image, the other a large image. You want the latter position.)

You need to make a pair of slits. This can be done by painting a microscope slide with black paint and, when dry, ruling two narrow, parallel lines close together as in Fig. 7.40. Put your slits in a suitable holder just behind the lens. You may have to cut out stray light with an improvised barrier.

Microscope slide painted black

About $\frac{1}{4}$ mm

Slits ruled through paint with razor blade

Fig. 7.40   The double slits

What do you see on the screen? Can you *explain* what you see?

7.16   A whole family of waves

In Chapter 1 you learnt about radiation energy. You saw that there is a large family consisting of different sorts of radiation, and that this family is called the **electromagnetic spectrum**. Both light and radar waves are members of this family.

With all the members of this family the energy is carried by waves, but the wavelength and frequency is different for each member. The photographs in Fig. 1.23 gave you clues about some members of this family. The clues represented the following:

radio waves
TV waves
radar waves
infrared waves
visible waves
ultraviolet waves
X-rays

The wavelength becomes smaller as you go down this list. You can see that it is a useful and important family, which is one reason that physicists need to understand waves.

Is there any important kind of energy that is carried by waves that are *not* a member of this family?

SUMMARY

Now that you have finished studying this chapter on waves, there are a number of things that you should know or be able to do.

1 You should:
  a) know the difference between a longitudinal and transverse wave;
  b) know an example of each kind of wave;
  c) be able to set up a ripple tank;
  d) be able to use a stroboscope to 'freeze' the motion of moving waves;
  e) be able to draw neat diagrams of what you see the waves doing in a ripple tank;
  f) know the rules of reflection for both straight and circular waves;
  g) know what refraction is, and be able to explain how it happens;
  h) know that waves diffract when they pass through a gap;
  i) know what difference the width of the gap makes to the amount of diffraction;
  j) be able to explain how interference occurs;
  k) know what evidence there is to suggest that light consists of waves.

2 You should know what each of the following is, or what each does:

wave	hertz
ripple	oscillator
pulse	micro-waves
wavelength	(radar waves)
frequency	electromagnetic
	spectrum

3 These are some of the other words that have been used in this chapter. You should know what each word means.

becalmed	evidence
destruction	dimension
transfer	constructive
continuous	destructive
slew	

FURTHER QUESTIONS

1 Look again at Fig. 7.2.
  a) As these waves spread out their amplitude becomes smaller. What is meant by the 'amplitude' of a wave?
  b) Explain why the amplitude becomes smaller.
  c) Do you think the water wave eventually vanishes, or do you think that, if the lake was big enough, the wave would keep going for ever?

2 a) Fig. 7.41(a) shows two waves approaching each other on a stretched spring. Draw two more diagrams to show what the spring will look like:
   i) as the waves meet;
   ii) a short time after the waves have met.

(a)

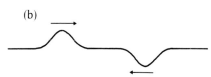
(b)

Fig. 7.41

  b) Fig. 7.41(b) shows a slightly different pair of waves. Draw another two diagrams showing the same things as in part (a).

3 The ripple tank in Fig. 7.10 shows a lamp above the water so that the ripples can cast shadows on the floor. But water is clear and transparent, so

133

how can it cast shadows? (Think of the shape of the water surface as the wave crosses the tank, and then think of what you know about rays of light.)

4 Fig. 7.42(a) shows a circular wave spreading out from a point O on a ripple tank. It is just about to hit a barrier AB. The next diagram shows part of the wave some time later. Copy this diagram and complete it, showing what has happened to the part of the wave that has been reflected. Mark

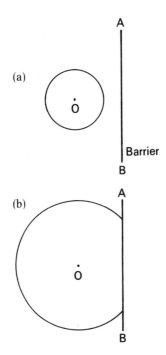

(a)

(b)

Barrier

Fig. 7.42

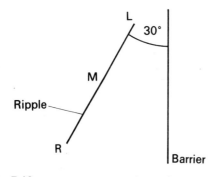

L
30°
M
Ripple
R
Barrier

Fig. 7.43

carefully on your diagram the place from which this reflected wave appears to be spreading.

5 Fig. 7.43 shows a straight wave heading towards a reflecting barrier, making an angle of 30° to the barrier. Draw three more diagrams to show what the wave will look like when:
a) end L has just reached the barrier;
b) the middle bit M has just reached the barrier;
c) The end R has just reached the barrier.
In each case mark on your diagram any angles that you know to be 30°.

6 A wagon wheel in a 'western' film has 12 spokes, all identical. The wheel goes round once a second.
a) If this wheel is looked at through a stroboscope with one slit, which is also being turned once a second, the wagon wheel appears stationary. Why is this?
b) The wagon wheel also appears stationary if the stroboscope has two slits, three slits or four slits, and is turning once a second. Explain why.
c) When you see a film of the turning wagon wheel, you see 24 pictures a second—like looking through a 24 slit stroboscope turning once a second. The 12 spoke wheel then appears to have 24 spokes, but still appears stationary. Explain why.
d) For each of the examples above, say whether the wagon wheel would still appear stationary if one of the spokes was painted red and the others were all painted white.

7 The diagram in Fig. 7.44 represents straight ripples crossing a ripple tank from left to right. A straight-sided glass plate has been put in one part of the tank to make the water in that part shallower.
a) Copy the diagram and draw a line to show where the edge of the plate is.
b) What is the wavelength of the

Direction of movement of waves

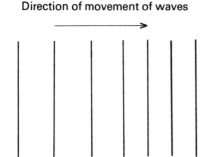

Fig. 7.44

Fig. 7.46

a) Copy the diagram and label a *crest* and a *trough*.
b) Mark on your diagram a distance equal to the wavelength of the wave.
c) Suppose someone standing in the waves counts 5 waves going past every second, what is the frequency of the waves?
d) If the wavelength of each wave is 2 cm, and 5 waves go past every second, how far away is the first wave to go past the person after 1 second?
e) What is the speed of the waves?
f) What is the speed of waves which have a wavelength of 3 cm and a frequency of 10 Hz (10 waves per second)?
g) Physicists often use the Greek letter λ (lambda) to represent the wavelength of waves. What is the speed

waves in the deep water? (Use a ruler).
c) What is the wavelength of the waves in the shallow water?
d) Have the waves speeded up or slowed down as they went from deep to shallow water?
8 Fig. 7.45 shows four kinds of barrier in a ripple tank. In each case, straight waves of wavelength 1 cm are approaching the barriers from the left. Copy the diagrams and, in each case, draw several waves to the right of the barrier to show what the waves do as they pass the barrier.
9 Fig. 7.46 shows the side view of a wave.

Fig. 7.45

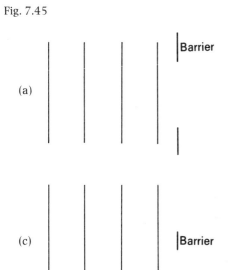

(a)

(c)

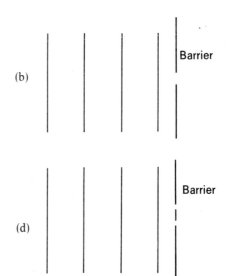

(b)

(d)

of waves of wavelength λ cm and of frequency f Hz?

10 Fig. 7.47 shows a ripple tank which is not quite level. A ripple was started at O. The diagram shows the shape of the ripple some time later.
a) Explain why the ripple has this shape.
b) Which side of the tank is the higher side? Give a reason for your answer.

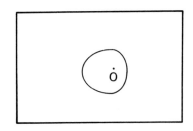

Fig. 7.47

INDEX